THE THEOLOGY OF THE BOOK OF AMOS

In modern times, Amos has come to be considered one of the most important prophets, mainly for his uncompromising message about social justice. This book provides a detailed exploration of this theme and other important elements of the theology underlying the book of Amos. It also includes chapters on the text itself, providing a critical assessment of how the book came to be, the original message of Amos and his circle, which parts of the book may have been added by later scribes, and the finished form of the book. The author also considers the book's reception in ancient and modern times by interpreters as varied as rabbis, the Church Fathers, the Reformers, and liberation theologians. Throughout, the focus is on how to read the book of Amos holistically to understand the organic development of the prophet's message through the many stages of the book's development and interpretation.

John Barton is Oriel and Laing Professor of the Interpretation of Holy Scripture, University of Oxford. He is the author of numerous monographs, including *Amos's Oracles against the Nations* (1980), *The Spirit and the Letter: Studies in the Biblical Canon* (1997), and *The Nature of Biblical Criticism* (2007).

OLD TESTAMENT THEOLOGY

GENERAL EDITORS

Brent A. Strawn
Associate Professor of Old Testament
Candler School of Theology, Emory University

Patrick D. Miller
Charles T. Haley Professor of Old Testament Theology, Emeritus
Princeton Theological Seminary

This series aims to remedy the deficiency of available published material on the theological concerns of the Old Testament books. Here, specialists explore the theological richness of a given book at greater length than is usually possible in the introductions to commentaries or as part of other Old Testament theologies. They are also able to investigate the theological themes and issues of their chosen books without being tied to a commentary format or to a thematic structure provided from elsewhere. When complete, the series will cover all the Old Testament writings and will thus provide an attractive, and timely, range of short texts around which courses can be developed.

PUBLISHED VOLUMES

The Theology of the Book of Genesis, R. W. L. Moberly
The Theology of the Book of Jeremiah, Walter Brueggemann

FORTHCOMING VOLUMES

The Theology of the Book of Exodus, Dennis T. Olson
The Theology of the Book of Leviticus, Brent A. Strawn
The Theology of the Book of Ecclesiastes, J. Gerald Janzen
The Theology of the Book of Daniel, Anathea Portier-Young

THE THEOLOGY OF THE
BOOK OF AMOS

JOHN BARTON

University of Oxford

CAMBRIDGE
UNIVERSITY PRESS

CAMBRIDGE UNIVERSITY PRESS
Cambridge, New York, Melbourne, Madrid, Cape Town,
Singapore, São Paulo, Delhi, Mexico City

Cambridge University Press
32 Avenue of the Americas, New York, NY 10013-2473, USA

www.cambridge.org
Information on this title: www.cambridge.org/9780521671750

First published 2012

Printed in the United States of America

A catalog record for this publication is available from the British Library.

Library of Congress Cataloging in Publication data
Barton, John, 1948–
The theology of the book of Amos / John Barton.
p.   cm. – (Old Testament theology)
Includes bibliographical references and index.
ISBN 978-0-521-85577-8 (hardback) – ISBN 978-0-521-67175-0 (paperback)
1. Bible. O.T. Amos – Criticism, interpretation, etc.   2. Bible. O.T.
Amos – Theology.   I. Title.
BS1585.52.B37   2012
224′.806–dc23   2011039686

ISBN 978-0-521-85577-8 Hardback
ISBN 978-0-521-67175-0 Paperback

For my father, Bernard Barton

Contents

General Editors' Preface

Some years ago, Cambridge University Press, under the editorship of James D. G. Dunn, initiated a series entitled *New Testament Theology*. The first volumes appeared in 1991 and the series was brought to completion in 2003. For whatever reason, a companion series that would focus on the Old Testament/Hebrew Bible was never planned or executed. The present series, *Old Testament Theology*, is intended to rectify this need.

The reasons for publishing *Old Testament Theology* are not, however, confined solely to a desire to match *New Testament Theology*. Instead, the reasons delineated by Dunn that justified the publication of *New Testament Theology* continue to hold true for *Old Testament Theology*. These include, among other things, the facts that (1) given faculty and curricular structures in many schools, the theological study of individual Old Testament writings is often spotty at best; (2) most exegetical approaches (and commentaries) proceed verse by verse such that theological interests are in competition with, if not completely eclipsed by, other important issues, whether historical, grammatical, or literary; and (3) commentaries often confine their discussion of a book's theology to just a few pages in the introduction. The dearth of materials focused exclusively on a particular book's theology may be seen as a result of factors like these; or, perhaps, it is the cause of such factors. Regardless, as Dunn concluded, without adequate theological resources, there is little incentive for teachers or students to engage the theology of specific books; they must be content with what are mostly general overviews. Perhaps the most serious problem resulting from all this is that students are at a disadvantage, even incapacitated, when it comes to the matter of integrating their study of the Bible with other courses in religion and theology. There is, therefore, an urgent need for a series to bridge the gap between the too-slim theological précis and the too-full commentary where theological concerns are lost among many others.

All of these factors commend the publication of *Old Testament Theology* now, just as they did for *New Testament Theology* more than two decades ago. Like its sister series, *Old Testament Theology* is a place where Old Testament scholars can write at greater length on the theology of individual biblical books and may do so without being tied to the linear, verse-by-verse format of the commentary genre or a thematic structure of some sort imposed on the text from outside. Each volume in the series seeks to describe the biblical book's theology as well as to engage the book theologically – that is, each volume intends to *do* theology through and with the biblical book under discussion, as well as delineate the theology contained within it. Among other things, theological engagement with the composition includes paying attention to its contribution to the canon and appraising its influence on and reception by later communities of faith. In these ways, *Old Testament Theology* seeks to emulate its New Testament counterpart.

In the intervening years since *New Testament Theology* was first conceived, however, developments have taken place in the field that provide still further reasons for the existence of *Old Testament Theology*; these have impact on how the series is envisioned and implemented and also serve to distinguish it, however slightly, from its companion series. Three developments in particular are noteworthy:

1. *The present hermeneutical climate,* often identified (rightly or wrongly) as "postmodern," is rife with possibility and potential for new ways of theologizing about scripture and its constituent parts. Theologizing in this new climate will of necessity look (and be) different from how it has ever looked (or been) before.

2. *The ethos change in the study of religion, broadly, and in biblical studies in particular.* No longer are the leading scholars in the field only Christian clergy, whether Catholic priests or mainline Protestant ministers. Jewish scholars and scholars of other Christian traditions are every bit as prominent, as are scholars of non- or even anti-confessional stripe. In short, now is a time when "Old Testament Theology" must be conducted without the benefits of many of the old consensuses and certainties, even the most basic ones relating to epistemological framework and agreed-upon interpretative communities along with their respective traditions.

3. Finally, recent years have witnessed *a long-overdue rapprochement among biblical scholars, ethicists, and systematic theologians.* Interdisciplinary studies between these groups are now regularly published, thus furthering and facilitating the need for books that make the theology of scripture widely available for diverse publics.

In brief, the time is ripe for a series of books that will engage the theology of specific books of the Old Testament in a new climate for a new day. The result will not be programmatic, settled, or altogether certain. Despite that – or, in some ways, *because* of that – it is hoped that *Old Testament Theology* will contain highly useful volumes that are ideally poised to make significant contributions on a number of fronts including (a) the ongoing discussion of biblical theology in confessional and nonconfessional mode as well as in postmodern and canonical contexts, (b) the theological exchange between Old Testament scholars and those working in cognate and disparate disciplines, and (c) the always-pressing task of introducing students to the theology of the discrete canonical unit: the biblical books themselves.

Brent A. Strawn
Candler School of Theology, Emory University

Patrick D. Miller
Princeton Theological Seminary, Emeritus

Preface

Of all the Minor Prophets, Amos has been of the most interest in modern times. This is partly because he was evidently the earliest of the "classical prophets" of Israel, but also because his message of divine judgment on social wrongdoing has resonated with many modern readers. My own conviction is that Amos should be seen as Israel's first theologian – the first to scrutinize critically the religious traditions of his people. Short as his book is, it fully justifies a place in the present series.

I have been interested in Amos since my student days. My doctoral thesis in 1974, entitled "The Relation of God to Ethics in the Eighth-Century Prophets," devoted considerable space to Amos, and I subsequently published a revised version of one chapter as *Amos's Oracles against the Nations*.[1] I have often taught the book of Amos for students at Oxford, either singly or as part of general courses on the prophets. Some of the ideas in this book were presented in outline in a paper to the Oxford Old Testament Seminar that was later published.[2]

---

[1] John Barton, *Amos's Oracles against the Nations* (SOTSMS 6; Cambridge: Cambridge University Press, 1980); reprinted in idem, *Understanding Old Testament Ethics* (Louisville: Westminster John Knox, 2003).

[2] John Barton, "The Theology of Amos," in *Prophecy and the Prophets in Ancient Israel: Proceedings of the Oxford Old Testament Seminar* (ed. John Day; LHBOTS 531; London: T & T Clark, 2010), 188–201.

I am indebted to the Theology Faculty Board in Oxford, which granted me a sabbatical term to work on this book, and to the staff of the Theology Faculty Library for a lot of help with bibliographical matters.

I am most grateful to the series editors, Brent Strawn and Patrick Miller, for their exceptionally careful work on my manuscript and for many suggestions for improvement. Please note that biblical citations are taken from the NRSV, unless otherwise indicated.

My wife Mary has been, as always, a great support while I have been working on this project. It is a great pleasure to dedicate the book to my father, Bernard Barton, on his 96th birthday. He continues to be interested in my work and will enjoy seeing a new book.

John Barton
Oriel College, Oxford
22 September 2010

Abbreviations

AB	Anchor Bible
AJSL	*American Journal of Semitic Languages and Literature*
ANET	James B. Pritchard, ed., *Ancient Near Eastern Texts Relating to the Old Testament*, 3rd ed. (Princeton: Princeton University Press, 1969)
AOAT	Alter Orient und Altes Testament
BCE	Before Common Era
BEvT	Beiträge zur evangelischen Theologie
BIS	Biblical Interpretation Series
BS	Biblical Seminar
BZ	*Biblische Zeitschrift*
BZAW	Beihefte zur Zeitschrift für die alttestamentliche Wissenschaft
CE	Common Era
CBQMS	Catholic Biblical Quarterly Monograph Series
ConBOT	Coniectanea biblica: Old Testament Series
CurBS	*Currents in Research: Biblical Studies*
EvT	*Evangelische Theologie*
FRLANT	Forschungen zur Religion und Literatur des Alten und Neuen Testaments

JBL	*Journal of Biblical Literature*
JJS	*Journal of Jewish Studies*
JSJSup	Journal for the Study of Judaism Supplement Series
JSOT	*Journal for the Study of the Old Testament*
JSOTSup	Journal for the Study of the Old Testament Supplement Series
JSS	*Journal of Semitic Studies*
LCL	Loeb Classical Library
LHBOTS	Library of Hebrew Bible/Old Testament Studies
LXX	The Septuagint
NRSV	New Revised Standard Version
NTT	*Norsk Teologisk Tidsskrift*
OTL	Old Testament Library
OtSt	Oudtestamentische Studiën
SBL	Society of Biblical Literature
SBLSymS	Society of Biblical Literature Symposium Series
SOTSMS	Society for Old Testament Studies Monograph Series
TRE	*Theologische Realenzyklopädie*
UF	*Ugarit-Forschungen*
v(v).	verse(s)
VT	*Vetus Testamentum*
VTSup	Supplements to Vetus Testamentum
WMANT	Wissenschaftliche Monographien zum Alten und Neuen Testament
ZAW	*Zeitschrift für die alttestamentliche Wissenschaft*

CHAPTER 1

Amos: The Critical Issues

A study devoted to the "The Theology of the *Book* of Amos" sounds as though it is meant to bypass the issues that have normally been the preserve of "the historical-critical method" – issues about the historical origins of the book, the context in which the prophet lived and worked, and the possibility of additions and changes to his original words. Contemporary biblical study has rightly put back on the agenda the need to interpret the finished product, the book as it lies before us when we open a Bible, and not to spend all our energies on "genetic" questions about how the book came to be, or on trying to identify an original core. But these conventional critical issues cannot be easily bypassed. Most books in the Old Testament are almost certainly the result of a long period of compilation, and the various stages through which they passed have implications for their meaning even as they now stand. In turn, intuitions about their meaning often condition our hypotheses about how they came to be. So we cannot avoid discussing historical-critical matters as a prelude to trying to analyze the theology of this prophetic book. In point of fact, this, too, is part of the mandate of the present series in which the present book is appearing.

The interwovenness of interpretative and critical issues can be seen most clearly if we begin with the most extreme critical positions. There are still scholars who defend the derivation of the entire book, or all but a few small fragmentary additions, from the eighth-century prophet Amos himself: examples include John H. Hayes and Shalom M. Paul.[1] For them, the prophet delivered a message to both the Hebrew kingdoms, which included both judgment to come and a following period of peace and prosperity – which is how the message of most biblical prophets appears in the books as we now have them. In this view, because it is quite thinkable that Amos would have uttered this combined message of judgment and hope, there is no reason to "delete" (to use the older critical vocabulary) the "epilogue" in 9:11–15 from the book as a later addition. At the opposite end of the spectrum, we have the work of Reinhard G. Kratz, who argues that scarcely any of the words attributed to Amos go back to the prophet himself.[2] All of the prophets, in Kratz's view, were basically supportive of the regimes under which they prophesied, as was normal throughout the ancient Near East. Consequently, almost all Amos's words of judgment must be secondary, which effectively removes nearly all of the book from serious consideration as a deposit of the prophet's teaching.

It is clear in both cases – those of the extreme optimism and extreme pessimism – that critical and interpretative issues are inextricably bound together. So we must begin by examining the book in the light of modern attempts to date and place the various oracles of which it is composed.

---

[1]   John H. Hayes, *Amos, the Eighth-Century Prophet: His Times and His Preaching* (Nashville: Abingdon, 1988); Shalom M. Paul, *Amos: A Commentary on the Book of Amos* (ed. F. M. Cross; Hermeneia; Minneapolis: Fortress, 1991).

[2]   Reinhard G. Kratz, "Die Worte des Amos von Tekoa," in *Propheten in Mari, Assyrien und Israel* (eds. M. Köckert and M. Nissinen; FRLANT 201; Göttingen: Vandenhoeck & Ruprecht, 2003), 54–89.

Hayes and Kratz do indeed represent opposite ends of a spectrum, but the majority of biblical scholars stand somewhere in between. For most, the book does genuinely go back in its core to the eighth-century prophet Amos, but this core has been expanded at various times to produce the book we have today. In what follows, we will work our way along the spectrum, beginning with those who think the book substantially the work of Amos.

COMPOSITIONAL THEORIES

Option 1: Most of the Book Comes from Amos

Many commentators in modern times have seen the book as in essentials the work of the prophet Amos. According to 1:1 and 7:10, Amos worked in the reign of Jeroboam II in the mid-eighth century BCE. He came from Tekoa (Khirbet Teqû'), five miles south of Bethlehem, and thus in the kingdom of Judah, but his prophetic activity, which may have lasted only a short time, was exercised in the northern kingdom of Israel, especially at the sanctuary of Bethel. This was a period of prosperity for both kingdoms, under the stable rule of Jeroboam II (789–748) and Uzziah (785–733) respectively. Peaceful times lasted until 745, which saw the rise of Assyria under Tiglath-pileser III, who would begin the military campaigns that led to the eventual demise of the northern kingdom and the decline of Judah into a minor state. So Amos must have worked some time before 745, since, though he predicts disaster for the north, there is no sign that it has yet begun, and he implies that the nation is living in comfort, with the only recent military activity having resulted in victories against Aram.

The Arameans of Damascus had been a constant threat to Israel during the ninth century, but had been checked by the Assyrian king Adadnirari III (810–783) at the beginning of the eighth century, and so were not a major problem for Israel again. The Assyrians were for a time held in check by the rising power of Urartu to their north, under Sardur III (810–743). Israel, if we are to believe the testimony of the book of Amos, thus enjoyed an "Indian summer" for the first half of the eighth century. Not only were the Arameans no longer a threat, but Israel regained towns in Transjordan from them. We learn this from Amos 6:13:

> you who rejoice in Lo-debar,
>> who say, "Have we not by our own strength
>> taken Karnaim for ourselves?"

Internally the country enjoyed prosperity. According to the book of Amos, the lifestyle of the ruling classes became, at least compared with what had preceded it, positively luxurious, with comfortable houses adorned with ivory:

> I will tear down the winter house as well as the summer house;
>> and the houses of ivory shall perish. (3:15)

> you have built houses of hewn stone,
>> but you shall not live in them;
> you have planted vineyards,
>> but you shall not drink their wine. (5:11)

> Alas for those who lie on beds of ivory,
>> and lounge on their couches,
> and eat lambs from the flock,
>> and calves from the stall;
> who sing idle songs to the sound of the harp,
>> and like David improvise on instruments of music;
> who drink wine from bowls,
>> and anoint themselves with the finest oils. (6:4–6)

This picture of luxury is supported to a great extent from archaeological excavations at Samaria. Whether Israel in this period was as hedonistic or self-indulgent as Amos suggests, we cannot tell: prophets are unlikely to underestimate the self-indulgence of their hearers, and luxury by ancient Israelite standards would probably seem fairly austere to a modern Westerner. But there is no reason to doubt that Amos was faced with a people living comfortably and without immediate fear of war.

Probably a majority of scholars believe, and always have believed, that most of the oracles preserved in the book of Amos reflect this period and are, as it used to be put, "authentic" – that is, they reflect the genuine words of the prophet himself. This is not necessarily to say that he wrote them down himself, as in the old designation of the prophets whose books appear in the Old Testament as so-called "writing prophets." Even on a conservative view of the authenticity of the sayings, most would probably assume that they were compiled by disciples or scribes, since Amos (like Socrates or Jesus) taught orally rather than in writing. But the eighth century provides such a congenial context for much of the teaching preserved in the book of Amos that there seems little reason to think it does not go back to the prophet himself. Paul even thinks that the arrangement of the book is Amos's own arrangement:

> Amos blended his new teaching with time-honored tradition in a very polished and artistic fashion. The book itself is a composite of independent collections with a well-organized structure arranged according to common literary genres.[3]

Francis I. Andersen and David Noel Freedman argue that the prophet's activity went through three stages, from each of which a significant body of oracles derive:[4]

(1) In chapters 5 and 6, and in the first two visions of chapter 7 (7:1–6) the prophet called the people to repent.

---

[3] Paul, *Amos*, 4–6.
[4] Francis I. Andersen and David N. Freedman, *Amos: A New Translation with Notes and Commentary* (AB 24A; New York: Doubleday, 1989).

(2) Chapters 3–4, chapters 1–2, and the next two visions in chapters 7–8 (7:7–8:3) proclaim that judgment will inevitably fall because there has been no repentance.

(3) And, finally, in 8:4–14 and 9:1–6 a special judgment is pronounced on the leaders of society.

For Andersen and Freedman, the book is thus a collection of "sermons," rather than an assemblage of small units.

For those scholars who defend the integrity of the whole, or nearly the whole, book, it often seemed necessary to present the theological ideas as not only coherent but also consistent. And yet there appear on the face of it to be real tensions in the book. For example, Amos 3:2 seems to assert the special election of Israel by YHWH:

> You only have I known of all the families of the earth;
> therefore I will punish you for all your iniquities

whereas 9:7 appears to deny it by putting the exodus of Israel from Egypt on a par with the origins of other nations:

> Are you not like the Ethiopians to me,
>   O people of Israel? says the LORD.
> Did I not bring up Israel from the land of Egypt,
>   and the Philistines from Caphtor and the Arameans from Kir?

Or Amos 7:1–6 speaks of YHWH "repenting" of his intention to destroy Israel ("It shall not be," says the LORD), but 7:7–9 announces that there will be no forgiveness:

> See, I am setting a plumb line in the midst of my people Israel;
>   I will never again pass them by;
> the high places of Isaac shall be made desolate,
>   and the sanctuaries of Israel shall be laid waste,
>   and I will rise against the house of Jeroboam with the sword.

If all the oracles go back to Amos himself, some way needs to be found of reconciling or explaining these discrepancies. One is to suggest that the prophet changed his mind over time, or, as he would have perhaps put it, he received new revelations from God that contradicted earlier ones. Ernst Würthwein proposed that Amos began life as a cultic prophet who was originally, in accordance with a standard prophetic role, a preacher of blessings for Israel, and it is from that period that the more hopeful material derives.[5] Amos fulfilled this role by interceding for Israel, and believed that Yhwh was telling him that the people would accordingly be forgiven. But later, he stepped out of role when he became convinced that the time for divine forbearance had passed and that only judgment remained, and that is when Amos added his oracles of divine destruction such as we find in the later visions of 7:7–9 and chapter 8.

Even scholars who defend most of the book as authentic tend to accept one of the oldest critical judgments – namely, that the "epilogue" of the book is a late addition:

> On that day I will raise up the booth of David that is fallen,
> and repair its breaches,
>> and raise up its ruins,
>> and rebuild it as in the days of old;
> in order that they may possess the remnant of Edom
>> and all the nations who are called by my name.
>> says the LORD who does this.
>
> The time is surely coming, says the LORD,
>> when the one who ploughs shall overtake the one who reaps,
>> and the treader of grapes the one who sows the seed;
> the mountains shall drip sweet wine,
>> and all the hills shall flow with it.

---

[5] See Ernst Würthwein, "Amos-Studien," *ZAW* 62 (1949–1950): 10–52.

> I will restore the fortunes of my people Israel,
> > and they shall rebuild the ruined cities and inhabit them;
> they shall plant vineyards and drink their wine,
> > and they shall make gardens and eat their fruit.
> I will plant them upon their land,
> > and they shall never again be plucked up
> > out of the land that I have given them,
> > > > says the LORD your God. (Amos 9:11–15)

Julius Wellhausen famously caught the difference between this passage and the bulk of the book by saying that it spoke of "roses and lavender instead of blood and iron."[6] Nevertheless, there are those who accept it as authentically part of Amos's message. Note, for example, Hayes's assessment:

> The historical context presupposed by the text and its allu-sions synchronize perfectly with what has been seen elsewhere in Amos, and with what can be reconstructed from other Old Testament texts. The text presupposes the troubled existence but not the demise of the house of David ... The uniqueness of the terminology in verse 11 argues for the text's authentic-ity. References to the booth of David occur nowhere else in Scripture. One would assume that a redactor adding a complete passage rather than merely glossing an existing text would have employed traditional terminology.[7]

To be sure, Amos was a southerner himself, and may well have seen the future as lying with Judah after the northern kingdom had been obliterated. Nevertheless, most scholars see the passage as an addition, probably reflecting the exilic or postexilic age when the line of David had ended – one that expressed the hope that it

---

[6] Julius Wellhausen, *Skizzen und Vorarbeiten 5: Die kleinen Propheten über-setzt und erklärt* (3rd ed.; Berlin: Reimer, 1898), 96: "Rosen und Lavendel statt Blut und Eisen."

[7] Hayes, *Amos*, 226.

would be restored, and this must mean that it does not come from Amos himself.

A great deal depends here on presuppositions about what is likely in the preservation of prophetic sayings. Some scholars, especially those influenced by the mid-twentieth-century, predominantly Scandinavian, emphasis on the reliability of oral transmission, have argued that the prophet's disciples probably transmitted his words faithfully to later generations, and, consequently, we have real access to his *ipsissima verba*.[8] Others, like Paul and Hayes, think in terms of the prophet himself as to some extent a highly literate person. Amos was no desert-dwelling, hairy seer like Elijah, but a sophisticated and educated man who could use clever literary devices, and who may well have been in the literal sense a "writing prophet." For example, Amos parodies the lament form in 5:1:

> Hear this word that I take up over you in lamentation,
>   O house of Israel:
> Fallen, no more to rise,
>   is maiden Israel;
> forsaken on her land,
>   with no one to raise her up

Here, the *qinah* form (a 3 + 2 beat pattern, common in lament texts such as Lamentations) is used to lament over an Israel that does not see itself as at all dead. Or again, in the oracles against the nations, Amos uses the form of the "numerical saying" known from Proverbs (see, e.g., Prov 30:18, 21, 24, 29):

> For three transgressions of Damascus,
>   and for four, I will not revoke the punishment.
>   (Amos 1:3; cf. 1:6, 9, 11, 13; 2:1, 4, 6)

---

[8]   See Erling Hammershaimb, *The Book of Amos: A Commentary* (Oxford: Blackwell, 1970).

And in 3:4–5, we find a parody of a priestly instruction or *torah*, in which the prophet sarcastically urges the people to sin by offering sacrifice:

> Come to Bethel – and transgress;
> > to Gilgal – and multiply transgression;
> bring your sacrifices every morning,
> > your tithes every three days;
> bring a thank-offering of leavened bread,
> > and proclaim freewill-offerings, publish them,
> > for so you love to do, O people of Israel!
> > > > > says the LORD.

If we see the prophet in this light, we will be disposed to think that the book may well derive from him rather than from disciples or anonymous scribes of later generations. Be that as it may, it remains true that the scholars who take this "high" view of the book's origin from Amos's own hand are in the minority.

Option 2: The Book Is the Result of a Process of Editing
The middle of our spectrum, and probably the most occupied area at present, is represented by those who think that, whatever Amos's own literary skills may or may not have been, the present book is the result of redaction – in truth, probably several stages of redaction.

The primary impetus to this way of thinking was represented by two influential works. The first, in 1965, was W. H. Schmidt's seminal paper on the deuteronomistic redaction of Amos, which argued that the book is not simply the product of one or more generations of disciples of the prophet but rather of the deuteronomistic movement, which during the exilic period in the sixth century took up the editing of prophetic literature with the consistent purpose of showing why the exile had occurred and how it had been foreseen by the great prophets.[9] Schmidt identified a number of places where deuteronomistic themes could be discerned, such as the following:

> Thus says the LORD:
> For three transgressions of Judah,
>   and for four, I will not revoke the punishment;
> because they have rejected the law of the LORD,
>   and have not kept his statutes,
> but they have been led astray by the same lies
>   after which their ancestors walked. (Amos 2:4)
>
> Surely the Lord GOD does nothing
>   without revealing his secret
>   to his servants the prophets. (Amos 3:7)
>
> Did you bring to me sacrifices and offerings the forty years in the
>   wilderness, O House of Israel? (Amos 5:25)

These additions stress the theme of obedience to the law (an idea that emerged later than the eighth century), the existence of a line of prophets (cf. 2 Kgs 24:2) among whom Amos is presumably numbered (whereas Amos himself denied that he was a prophet), and the non-sacrificial character of worship during the wilderness wanderings (which is assumed in Deuteronomy but was probably not believed in the time of Amos). Amos's own message would emerge more clearly, Schmidt believed, if these additions were removed.

The other major move toward a redactional model for the development of Amos can be found in Hans Walter Wolff's commentary of 1969, translated into English in 1977.[10] This analyzed the

---

[9] W. H. Schmidt, "Die deuteronomistische Redaktion des Amosbuches: Zu den theologischen Unterschieden zwischen dem Prophetenwort und seinem Sammler," *ZAW* 77 (1965): 168–192.

[10] Hans Walter Wolff, *Joel and Amos: A Commentary on the Books of the Prophets Joel and Amos* (trans. W. Janzen, S. D. McBride, Jr., and C. A. Muenchow; ed. S. D. McBride, Jr.; Hermeneia; Philadelphia: Fortress, 1977 [German orig.: 1969]).

book in detail and proposed a number of stages in its development. According to Wolff, the original core of the book, which goes back to the prophet himself, consisted of a number of the oracles now found in chapters 3–6 ("the words of Amos of Tekoa"), augmented by the prophet through the addition of the authentic five oracles against the nations, now located in chapters 1–2 (excluding those against Tyre and Edom, which many other scholars also regard as secondary), and the account of five visions in chapters 7–9. This is the extent of the prophet's own contribution to the book.

The next stage is represented by what Wolff calls "the old school of Amos" – oracles compiled by disciples but which in some cases at least are authentic memories of the prophet's actions and sayings. "[T]his old school of Amos still had at its disposal remembered deeds and sayings of the prophet which were transmitted as part of neither the 'words of Amos of Tekoa' nor the recorded cycles."[11] An example of this type of material is 7:10–17, Amos's contretemps with Amaziah, the priest of Bethel, which according to Wolff rests on eyewitness testimony but, since it is recounted in the third person, cannot be by Amos himself.

> Then Amaziah, the priest of Bethel, sent to King Jeroboam of Israel, saying, "Amos has conspired against you in the very center of the house of Israel; the land is not able to bear all his words. For thus Amos has said, 'Jeroboam shall die by the sword, and Israel must go into exile, away from his land.'"
>
> And Amaziah said to Amos, "O seer, go, flee away to the land of Judah, earn your bread there, and prophesy there; but never again prophesy at Bethel, for it is the king's sanctuary, and it is a temple of the kingdom."
>
> Then Amos answered Amaziah, "I am no prophet, nor a prophet's son; but I am a herdsman, and a dresser of sycomore

---

[11] Ibid., 108.

trees, and the LORD took me from following the flock, and the LORD said to me, 'Go, prophesy to my people Israel.'"

The "old school" of Amos was active in the years after the prophet's own activity ended, probably around the time of the Assyrian crisis for the northern kingdom in 735, since the editors seem to look back on Amos himself from a vantage point after the earthquake he had predicted and at a time when his oracles of judgment were beginning to come true. An illustrative example is found in 8:8:

> Shall not the land tremble on this account,
>   and everyone mourn who lives in it,
> and all of it rise like the Nile,
>   and be tossed about and sink again,
>   like the Nile of Egypt?

Here, Wolff suggests, "a threat is presented in the form of a question, such as never occurs in Amos's own oracles, but which is quite intelligible if it derived from the discussion of disciples about words of the master."[12] Similarly, 8:9–10 and 8:13–14 are also works of this school – dated very soon after Amos, but not actually from the prophet himself.

It is difficult to see how Wolff knows so much about the origin of these sayings, so as to be able to separate them as the work of immediate disciples rather than the words of Amos himself; nevertheless, the model of an "old school of Amos" seems inherently plausible.

The next stages involve additions to the words of Amos in scribal circles that no longer had a direct connection to the prophet himself. Wolff believes that one such expansion of the Amos material happened in the time of Josiah, in the seventh century. Amos

---

[12] Ibid.

had certainly prophesied against Bethel, but in the light of Josiah's destruction of the shrine there (see 2 Kgs 23:15–20), Amos's own words were expanded to include more anti-Bethel material, such as 5:6:

> Seek the LORD and live,
>> or he will break out against the house of Joseph like fire,
>> and it will devour Bethel, with no one to quench it.

It is at this stage that the three strophes of a hymn about the destructive power of YHWH were added at salient points in the prophet's words:

> For lo, the one who forms the mountains, creates the wind,
>> reveals his thoughts to mortals,
> makes the morning darkness,
>> and treads on the heights of the earth –
>> the LORD, the God of hosts, is his name! (Amos 4:13)

> The one who made the Pleiadies and Orion,
>> and turns deep darkness into the morning,
>> and darkens the day into night,
> who calls for the waters of the sea,
>> and pours them out on the surface of the earth,
> the LORD is his name,
> who makes destruction flash out against the strong,
>> so that destruction comes upon the fortress. (Amos 5:8–9)

> The Lord, GOD of hosts,
> he who touches the earth and it melts,
>> and all who live in it mourn,
> and all of it rises like the Nile,
>> and sinks again, like the Nile of Egypt;
> who builds his upper chambers in the heavens,
>> and founds his vault upon the earth;
> who calls for the waters of the sea,
>> and pours them out upon the surface of the erath –
> the LORD is his name. (Amos 9:5–6)

Wolff suggests that these "doxologies" "allow speculation that the 'Bethel-exposition' was associated with a concrete liturgical occasion at the Bethel sanctuary in the third decade before the end of the seventh century."[13]

Subsequent scholarship has not been confident that Wolff was correct in detecting a separate Josianic strand in the book – Jörg Jeremias, for example, who in general follows Wolff, assigns the material in the "Bethel-Exposition" to later strata.[14] He and most other commentators agree with Wolff, however, that there was a significant further edition of Amos in the sixth century – the deuteronomistic editing to which Schmidt drew attention. It is at this stage that a number of the most clearly non-Amos elements were added: for example, (i) the oracles against Tyre and Edom (1:9–12), which the circumstances at that time demanded, especially as Edom had now become the enemy of Judah by helping the Babylonians when they sacked Jerusalem (cf. Obadiah); and (ii) the idea that the prophets formed a line of succession (3:7) that had the function of trying to bring Israel back to Yhwh. The deuteronomistic editors thus make Amos relevant for the generation in exile, and present him as having foreseen not simply the Assyrian threat of the eighth century but the Babylonian attacks of their own time. It is this redactional layer that has in effect given the book its salient character, and the deuteronmists were also active in editing other prophetic books – perhaps nowhere is this clearer than in the book of Jeremiah.[15]

---

[13] Ibid., 112.

[14] Jörg Jeremias, *The Book of Amos: A Commentary* (trans. D. W. Stott; OTL; Louisville: Westminster John Knox, 1998 [German orig: 1995]).

[15] Cf. Ernest W. Nicholson, *Preaching to the Exiles: A Study of the Prose Tradition in the Book of Jeremiah* (Oxford: Blackwell, 1970); Robert P. Carroll, *From Chaos to Covenant: Uses of Prophecy in the Book of Jeremiah* (London: SCM, 1981).

Wolff's final stage of Amos's editing consists of the addition of the epilogue (9:11–15), which at some point after the exile was designed to make Amos prophesy the eventual restoration of Judah. By this time, all prophets were understood to have uttered words of comfort for Israel, and Amos was not permitted to be an exception.

Other scholars have worked with the same general principles as Wolff, thinking it certain that a core of authentic words have been augmented, altered, and supplemented in various ways, but differing as to the specific details. Wolff's separation of the "words of Amos from Tekoa" from the vision-cycle is developed in a different way by Ina Willi-Plein, who thinks the eighth-century collection contained the main oracles in 1–4, with the vision-cycle plus the account in 7:10–14 separate from it though still formed within the prophet's own lifetime.[16] The next edition, however, was made in the time of Manasseh (thus earlier than Wolff's Josianic redaction), and consisted of a reworking of the visions to produce chapters 5–9, which the deuteronomists then combined with chapters 1–4 in the exilic age. At this point, Willi-Plein's and Wolff's understandings of the book's redaction more or less coincide, though they have reached them by different routes. Willi-Plein then, like Wolff, supposes that there were further additions in postexilic times, some even of an apocalyptic type. Klaus Koch, on the other hand, makes more of the supposed Josianic phase, in which redactors took tradition-complexes that were already formed and combined them with some oral traditions; in this reconstruction, again the epilogue was added last.[17]

---

[16] Ina Willi-Plein, *Vorformen der Schriftexegese innerhalb des Alten Testaments: Untersuchungen zum literarischen Werden der auf Amos, Hosea und Micha zurückgehenden Bücher im hebräischen Zwölfprophetenbuch* (BZAW 123; Berlin: Walter de Gruyter, 1971).

[17] Klaus Koch, *Amos: Untersucht mit den Mitteln strukturaler Formgeschichte* (3 vols.; AOAT 30; Kevelaer: Butzon & Bercker and Neukirchen-Vluyn: Neukirchener Verlag, 1976).

Even more complex than Wolff's analysis is that of Dirk U. Rottzoll, who finds no fewer than twelve different strata in the book![18] As is generally true of this kind of "composition criticism," it is more or less impossible to falsify any of the theories proposed, but equally difficult to regard any of them as demonstrably true: they represent more or less plausible suggestions to deal with the observable diversity and inconsequentiality of much of the material in the book. While it seems hardly likely (*pace* Hayes and Paul) that the book of Amos is a deliberate composition planned by a single hand, it is almost equally unlikely that we will be able to trace its detailed development with anything more than reasonable guesses. In all this, we should not lose sight of the practicalities of the matter. Twelve editions means twelve scribes or groups of scribes rewriting a scroll and adding material to it, reshaping its order, and – crucially – adjusting its content in subtle ways to make fresh points each time the material is rearranged. This is not impossible, but it does imply learned circles with considerable time and energy to devote to the work, and plentiful supplies of writing materials. When we speak of "collections of tradition," we need to be clear whether we mean orally transmitted sayings and stories or scrolls containing written material; and if we mean the latter, we need to ask how they were stored and preserved, who had access to them, how free any scribe was to change them when copying them out, and who actually read them and in what context. Old Testament scholars ask these questions far too infrequently, and can easily produce free-floating hypotheses about the redaction and composition of books not anchored in the practical realities of ancient scroll production.[19]

[18] Dirk U. Rottzoll, *Studien zur Redaktion und Komposition des Amosbuches* (BZAW 243; Berlin: Walter de Gruyter, 1996).

[19] See further, Emanuel Tov, "Book-Scrolls in Israel in Pre-exilic Times," *JJS* 32 (1982): 161–173.

More recently, Tchavdar Hadjiev has undertaken a complete review (to which my own discussion is very much indebted) of the various theories about the composition of Amos, and has presented a persuasive model developing and refining the work of Wolff and Jeremias.[20] He suggests, as do many others, that the core of the book is the oracles in chapters 3–6, in which there is a ring composition in 5:1–17 (as nearly all agree),[21] and the materials on either side are also broadly chiastic from 4:1 to 6:7. Outside this block, however, he finds little concentricity, and he points to weaknesses in all the hypotheses that have found any. Probably, therefore, we should reckon with two phases of composition: an original compilation of 4:1–6:7 as a "ring," and then a second stage at which the rest of chapters 3–6 were added. This produced a first edition of Amos, which Hadjiev calls the "Repentance Scroll." Its "main aim is devastating criticism of the aristocracy of Northern Israel, focusing on their luxurious lifestyle (4:1–3; 6:1–7), attitude toward the cult (4:4–12; 5:18–24) and social and judicial abuses (5:1–17), exploring the interrelationship of these three leadership failures as well as their inevitable theological consequences – the impending destruction."[22] It is to this core text that most of the appeals to repentance belong – which may call in question the widespread idea that the original Amos did not preach repentance.[23] This corpus of material would make sense in the last decade of the northern kingdom, down to 722, when Israel had not yet fallen but was already being reduced to a rump state by Assyrian incursions. It incorporates genuine words of Amos, which his disciples had remembered.

[20] Tchavdar S. Hadjiev, *The Composition and Redaction of the Book of Amos* (BZAW 393; Berlin: Walter de Gruyter, 2009).
[21] See the discussion below.
[22] Hadjiev, *The Composition and Redaction of the Book of Amos*, 185.
[23] See the further discussion in Chapter 3 herein.

The Repentance Scroll, Hadjiev argues, went into a second edition in Judah after the fall of the North. A summary of its major themes for new readers is provided at 3:9–15:

> Proclaim to the strongholds in Ashdod,
>> and to the strongholds in the land of Egypt,
> and say, "Assemble yourselves on Mount Samaria,
>> and see what great tumults are within it,
>> and what oppressions are in its midst."
> They do not know how to do right, say the LORD,
>> those who store up violence and robbery in their strongholds.
> Therefore, thus says the Lord GOD:
> An adversary shall surround the land,
>> and strip you of your defense;
>> and your strongholds shall be plundered.
>
> Thus says the LORD: As the shepherd rescues from the mouth of the lion two legs, or a piece of an ear, so shall the people of Israel who live in Samaria be rescued, with the corner of a couch and part of a bed.
>
> Hear, and testify against the house of Jacob,
>> says the Lord GOD, the God of hosts:
> On the day I punish Israel for its transgressions,
>> I will punish the altars of Bethel,
> and the horns of the altar shall be cut off
>> and fall to the ground.
> I will tear down the winter house as well as the summer house;
>> and the houses of ivory shall perish,
> and the great houses shall come to an end,
>>>> says the LORD.

This edition presents the coming judgment as a military invasion (rather than an earthquake as in 6:11), and includes Judah in the predicted disaster (6:1). There is no future via repentance in this version of the oracles – the time for repentance has now passed, since the northern kingdom has (for the contemporary reader) already fallen.

There is then another collection of Amos material, consisting of the core five oracles against the nations (1:3–5; 1:6–8; 1:13–15; 2:1–3; 2:6–16), the five visions (7:1–3; 7:4–6; 7:7–9; 8:1–3; 9:1–4), the narrative in 7:10–17, and the oracles in 3:3–8, 9:7, and 9:9–10. This material also probably goes back to the prophet himself, at least in essentials, but has been edited to give the oracles a coherent shape, modeling the oracles against the nations on the pattern of the visions. The whole complex is an answer to the claim that "this evil will not come to us" (9:9–10). The story of Amos and Amaziah shows how people may react negatively to the prophet's message and how dire will be the consequences of doing so. This second collection also predates the fall of the North, and Hadjiev calls it the "Polemical Scroll"; it is probably to be dated between the earth-quake and military invasion by the Assyrians:

> The way in which the movement goes from earthquake to defeat and exile, with the stress being placed on the second, carries the implicit argument that the fulfilment of the first prediction of Amos is a sure proof that his other predictions concerning the defeat and exile will also come true. The aim of the compilers may have been to interpret the earthquake announced by Amos as the initial manifestation of Yahweh's judgment which was going to manifest itself in the future in the military defeat and exile which were also foretold by Amos.[24]

These two scrolls were then combined as part of a "Liturgical Redaction," when the "doxologies" were also added, probably to assist the use of the book in worship (hence *liturgical* redaction). This probably happened in the seventh century, and must have taken place in Judah.

Further redaction followed during the exile: the Tyre, Edom, and Judah oracles were added in chapters 1–2, 8:3–14 was inserted,

---

[24] Hadjiev, *The Composition and Redaction of the Book of Amos*, 198.

and the book was given a hopeful epilogue (9:7–15). The effect was to help explain the exile of Judah by accusing it of having ignored the law and the prophets, but also to give hope for restoration after judgment. Whereas Judah had been as bad as Edom, now she would rule over the Edomites, as in the (possibly idealized) remote past. The overall result was to produce a book in three parts: an introduction (chapters 1–2), the presentation of Israel's social and cultic sins as a transgression of the Law (chapters 3–6), and an attempt to show how Israel's rejection of Amos's prophetic word led to the final judgment (chapters 7–9). The redactions of the book show some affinities with the deuteronomistic school of thought, but they are not themselves on the whole deuteronomistic, evincing as they do some cultic and sacral concerns (note 2:7: "profane my holy name"; and 8:14 on the worship of "foreign" gods such as "Ashimah"). There were probably no postexilic redactional additions: the final audience was the impoverished Judean community in the land during the exile itself.

For Hadjiev, it is impossible to demonstrate that any words in the book definitely go back to Amos, but the very earliness of the major collections suggests that those who wrote them either were his disciples or at least were in close touch with his disciples. There is thus every probability that we have genuine evidence for the ideas of the prophet himself.

In sum, it might be observed that, in the Hayes/Paul model (Option 1), the theology of the book of Amos and the theology of the prophet Amos are essentially one and the same. In the models discussed in the present section (loosely connected as "Option 2"), these entities are clearly different: we need to speak of the theology of *each update of the words of Amos*, and these different theologies developed over time. It is not clear that any one of them is more "authoritative" for a modern reader than any other, though some readers might still accord a special place to the authentic words of the prophet himself and perhaps also to the finished product, the book as we now have it.[25] But, if Wolff was right, there was a seventh-century book of Amos that had its own integrity and, no doubt, its own theology. In what follows, I will not try to analyze the theological ideas of each redactional stage, but this is not because the task could not be carried out; rather, it is because I do not think the existence of these strata is demonstrated convincingly enough to make the task worthwhile. In principle, however, the second option indicates that there are many "theologies of Amos," and all might have something constructive to offer us. Indeed, even if the book were a unity, it might contain differing theological emphases; but this is more obviously the case if it is the product of a redaction by a number of different people.

Option 3: The Book Is a Deliberate Literary Production
Other theories about the composition of the book have thought less of the gradual addition of material to an original substratum and more of a careful compositional structure. Whereas reconstructions such as Wolff's imply a text that, each time it is recopied, receives additions, these theories propose that the editor(s) had a lot of materials, some perhaps authentic but some certainly not, which they arranged to make a skillful literary composition. Here, therefore, we meet primarily literary analysis of the book, often involving chiasmus or "ring-composition." The more skillful the composition, it is thought, the less likely it probably is to reflect genuine Amos traditions, and so the further we are from Hayes's position that the whole book goes back to the prophet. Of

---

[25] Cf., e.g., Jeremias, who in his commentary prints in italics material he thinks secondary, and expounds it rather little.

course, it is conceivable that the material is all from Amos even if its arrangement is secondary; or even that Amos himself arranged his own oracles to make a coherent pattern. But commentators who detect artistry in the arrangement have usually seen such as the work of an editor or editors.

Amos 3–6 is widely held to show evidence of having been edited so as to produce a "ring" or concentric structure. The central passage is 5:1–17, which itself is already chiastic or rather concentric in form, as can be seen from the following way of structuring it:[26]

A Hear this word that I take up over you in lamentation, O house of Israel:
Fallen, no more to rise,
    is maiden Israel;
forsaken on her land,
    with no one to raise her up.

For thus says the Lord GOD:
The city that marched out a thousand shall have a hundred left,
and that which marched out a hundred shall have ten left.

B For thus says the LORD to the house of Israel:
Seek me and live,
    but do not seek Bethel,
and do not enter into Gilgal
    or cross over to Beer-sheba;
for Gilgal shall surely go into exile,
    and Bethel shall come to nothing.
Seek the LORD and live,

---

[26] See J. de Waard, "The Chiastic Structure of Amos V,1–17," *VT* 27 (1977): 170–177; Rottzoll, *Studien zur Redaktion und Komposition des Amosbuches*; Paul R. Noble, "The Literary Structure of Amos: A Thematic Analysis," *JBL* 114 (1995): 209–226; and R. Bryan Widbin, "Center Structure in the Center Oracles of Amos," in *"Go to the Land I Will Show You": Studies in Honor of Dwight W. Young* (eds. J. E. Coleson and V. H. Matthews; Winona Lake: Eisenbrauns, 1996), 177–192; all suggest that chapters 3–6 are a ring composition. See also Hadjiev, *The Composition and Redaction of the Book of Amos*, 232.

or he will break out against the house of Joseph like fire,
and it will devour Bethel, with no one to quench it.

C   Ah, you that turn justice to wormwood,
        and bring righteousness to the ground!

    D   The one who made the Pleiades and Orion,
            and turns deep darkness into the morning,
            and darkens the day into night,
        who calls for the waters of the sea,
            and pours them out on the surface of the earth,
        the LORD is his name,
        who makes destruction flash out against the strong,
            so that destruction comes upon the fortress.

C′   They hate the one who reproves in the gate,
        and they abhor the one who speaks the truth.
    Therefore because you trample on the poor
        and take from them levies of grain,
    you have built houses of hewn stone,
        but you shall not live in them;
    you have planted pleasant vineyards,
        but you shall not drink their wine.
    For I know how many are your transgressions,
        and how great are your sins –
    you who afflict the righteous, who take a bribe,
        and push aside the needy in the gate.
    Therefore the prudent will keep silence in such a time,
        for it is an evil time.

B′   Seek good and not evil,
        that you may live;
    and so the LORD, the God of hosts, will be with you,
        just as you have said.
    Hate evil and love good,
        and establish justice in the gate;
    it may be that the LORD, the God of hosts,
        will be gracious to the remnant of Joseph.

A′   Therefore thus says the LORD, the God of hosts, the Lord:
    In all the squares there shall be wailing;

and in all the streets they shall say, "Alas! alas!"
They shall call the farmers to mourning,
and those skilled in lamentation, in wailing;
in all the vineyards there shall be wailing,
for I will pass through the midst of you,
says the LORD.

It is likely that most of the individual sayings here are older than their incorporation into the final pattern, since they do not match as exactly as we might expect them to do if they had been written specifically for that purpose. For example, v. 7 (= C) is much shorter than its equivalent, vv. 10–13 (= C′). Nevertheless, the arrangement does seem intentional, as Jeremias argues:

> [T]he reader is to traverse a conceptual progression both commencing and ending with the pitiless lament for the death of Israel (A/A′), because this people of God obstructed the implementation of justice (C/C′); this seemingly inflexible logic, however, is now unexpectedly interrupted by the insertion – between the lament and its justification – of a twofold summons to seek God, accompanied by the promise of life. This can only mean that one might, by following that summons, sunder the connection between sin and death (B/B′). Finally, in the middle – which always bears the main emphasis in ring compositions – this progression issues in praise of the God who both kills and bestows life (D).[27]

This is a lot to read out of the structure; nevertheless, as we will see later, the appeal to the God who "both kills and bestows life" is indeed a central feature of the theology of the book of Amos. We see here again how the composition history of the book and its interpretation go hand-in-hand and cannot be separated.

On either side of this ring composition, there are sections criticizing the cult (4:4–13 and 5:18–27); around these are attacks on

---

[27] Jeremias, *Amos*, 84–85.

the aristocracy who are living in luxury (4:1–3 and 6:1–7). This seems unlikely to be accidental, and argues for a strong redactional hand, and possibly for an author later than Amos himself, if there is justification for the widespread assumption that the exclusively "original" material was fragmentary and would not have naturally lent itself to arrangement into this convenient ring form.[28] It would be possible to argue that Amos himself structured his oracles in this way or even delivered them in a ring form – this is connected to the question of how much artistic skill we are prepared to ascribe to the prophet himself. But, again, those who have detected chiastic or ring compositions have generally thought of them as the work of later redactors, working with a mixture of authentic and inauthentic material.

What complicates the issue is that chapters 3–5 also manifest an alternative, more linear arrangement, with 3:1 and 5:1 dividing the center of the book into two parts: chapters 3–4 and chapters 5–6. Since either structure in some measure destroys the other, it seems that we must be dealing with two redactors who had different ideas about the structure, and it is difficult to decide which came first.

Others have noted that the five (authentic) oracles against the nations at the beginning of the book are paralleled by the five visions at the end. This arrangement also has chiastic features, as does the mention of the Arameans being exiled beyond Kir in 1:5, and the assertion that Kir is where they came from in 9:7. If the book was indeed structured in a ring form, then our attention should probably lie with its center, 5:7–10, which is a classic statement of

---

[28] Thus N. J. Tromp, "Amos V 1–17: Towards a Stylistic and Rhetorical Analysis," in *Prophets, Worship and Theodicy: Studies in Prophetism, Biblical Theology and Structural and Rhetorical Analysis and on the Place of Music in Worship: Papers Read at the Joint British–Dutch Old Testament Conference held at Woudschoten, 1982* (OtSt 23; Leiden: Brill, 1984), 65–85.

Amos's uncompromising message of doom. Moreover, recognizing a structure running from 1:3 to 9:8, as these observations imply, might also mean that the epilogue in 9:11–15 falls outside the confines of the book proper and is indeed a very late addition.

Finding a literary arrangement of this kind has two important possible implications. One is that reconstructing an "original" Amos becomes difficult because the material could have been manufactured to fit its present place in the structure. And if that is true, then the quest for "authentic" passages becomes rather hopeless. The other, which is clearly significant for our purposes in the present book, is that the meaning we attribute to the book is likely to be related to the structure we have discovered – as in the suggestion just made that its center lies in an oracle of judgment. Whereas the conventions of modern literature might lead us to think of the end as giving a clue to the meaning of the whole – and hence to see the book overall as climaxing in an oracle of blessing – attention to the ancient form of the ring composition shifts the weight to the center and suggests that the book as a whole should be read as primarily about doom.[29] Somewhat paradoxically, then, the reading prompted by this kind of literary analysis thus tends to chime in with the traditional critical reading in which the authentic Amos is seen primarily as a prophet of judgment.

The most advanced ring-composition theory is probably that of Rottzoll. In addition to believing that the book went through

[29] On ring composition, see Nathan Klaus, *Pivot Patterns in the Former Prophets* (JSOTSup 247; Sheffield: Sheffield Academic Press, 1999); and Jerome T. Walsh, *Style and Structure in Biblical Hebrew Narrative* (Collegeville, MN: Liturgical, 2001). John W. Welch, ed., *Chiasmus in Antiquity* (Hildesheim: Gerstenberger Verlag, 1981) contains a number of studies on the phenomenon in ancient texts. Note especially Yehuda Radday's contribution, "Chiasmus in Hebrew Biblical Narrative" (50–117).

twelve redactional stages, he also thinks that in the postexilic period it was edited again to produce one giant ring composition (though he then "deletes" any passages that do not fit it, which is, of course, a dubious enterprise!).

These literary models for the book are attractive in suggesting that it is coherent – just as coherent as on the assumption that it is all by Amos, as Paul argues. But the insight we gain from reading it is essentially insight into the mind of a late redactor, quite probably living in the Persian period, at some point after the exile.[30] If a similar analysis is practiced on other prophetic books, then a picture might emerge of how prophecy was understood in postexilic times. I have sketched some ideas about this in my book *Oracles of God*.[31] The effect of these late redactions was to obliterate the differences between the individual prophets, or at least greatly reduce them, and in studying the theology of the *book* of Amos, we will see that this is precisely what happened.

Option 4: "Amos" as a Later Invention
At the far end of the spectrum stand theories that portray the prophet Amos as very largely invented in later times, and the book as having little or no anchorage in the eighth century at all. Kratz's interpretation comes close to this. He is clear that there are a few sayings that probably do go back to the prophet himself: there really was a prophet called Amos who prophesied under Jeroboam II. But what that prophet said bore very little resemblance to the ideas the present book puts in his mouth. Amos was a prophet like other prophets in the ancient Near East, as known from Mari, for

---

[30] See Chapter 4 herein.
[31] John Barton, *Oracles of God: Perceptions of Ancient Prophecy in Israel after the Exile* (2nd ed.; New York: Oxford University Press, 2007 [1st ed.: 1986]).

example.[32] Like them, Amos sometimes warned that the nation would be unsuccessful in battle or would undergo various troubles; but at no point did he speak of the complete collapse of Israel or seek to undermine its institutions – no prophet ever did that, in reality. Kratz's interpretation is summarized as follows by Hadjiev:

> The historical Amos criticised the sins of the Samarian aristocracy and was able to predict the coming military threat to Israel. The tradition transformed that figure into the literary Amos – an uncompromising prophet of doom who proclaimed Yahweh's coming judgment on Israel on behalf of their sins.[33]

This invention of Amos happened in late preexilic times according to Kratz, but others have argued (following the far-sighted work of Edward Day and Walter H. Chapin in 1902)[34] that it was a work of the postexilic period. This is argued by James R. Linville and by Oswald Loretz – both of whom suggest that the deuteronomistic "redaction" identified by Schmidt and supported by Wolff is more or less the whole story: the prophet Amos was manufactured from whole cloth, in order to retroject into the eighth century the deuteronomistic picture of prophecy.[35] Even if there was someone of that name, his actual teaching is both irrecoverable and immaterial. Only the finished book exists, and it is simply a fiction, to

---

[32] Cf. Martti Nissinen, ed., *Prophecy in its Ancient Near Eastern Context: Mesopotamian, Biblical, and Arabian Perspectives* (SBLSymS 13; Atlanta: Society of Biblical Literature, 2000).

[33] Hadjiev, *The Composition and Redaction of the Book of Amos*, 10–11.

[34] Edward Day and Walter H. Chapin, "Is the Book of Amos Post-Exilic?," *AJSL* 18 (1902): 65–93.

[35] James R. Linville, "Amos among the 'Dead Prophets Society': Re-reading the Lion's Roar," *JSOT* 90 (2000): 55–77; Oswald Loretz, "Die Entstehung des Amos-Buches im Licht der Prophetien aus Mari, Assur, Ischchali und der Ugarit-Texte: Paradigmenwechsel in der Prophetenbuchforschung," *UF* 24 (1992): 179–215.

be read like other fictions of postexilic times (Jonah or Ruth, for
example). This is implied also in the work of Philip R. Davies,
who thinks that almost all the preexilic "traditions" of Israel were
invented after the exile.[36]

There are several problems with this very late dating for the
Amos traditions, well set out by Hadjiev.[37] As he argues, though
the message of Amos no doubt continued to be *relevant* in the
postexilic age, it is difficult to see it as having been *created* then.
The enemy who will destroy Israel is never named – as it is in later
works such as Jeremiah and Ezekiel – and exile is only one of the
aspects of the coming disaster: the language of earthquake does
not fit the Babylonian exile. There is no suggestion that Israel perceives itself as a weak victim; rather, the people think of the nation
as strong and prosperous, and it is only the prophet who sees it
as threatened by its enemies – wholly different from the exilic or
postexilic situation. Damascus is the main enemy identified by the
prophet, and it was no great power in the Assyrian, Babylonian, or
Persian periods. For a postexilic editor to have invented the conflict with Aram, such a person would have had to be writing exceptionally clever and accurate (historical) fiction. Furthermore, with
the exception of a few passages almost universally agreed to be
later additions, the book is directed to the northern kingdom of
Israel, which no longer existed after the eighth century. The oracles
against the nations in chapters 1–2 also make sense only in preexilic
times, however much they may have been added to and expanded
later. The Israel of the book of Amos has an army, a king, no foreign overlord; and it has recently recaptured two Transjordanian
towns from the Arameans, one of which, Qarnaim, became the

---

[36] Philip R. Davies, *In Search of "Ancient Israel"* (JSOTSup 148; Sheffield: JSOT
Press, 1992).

[37] Hadjiev, *The Composition and Redaction of the Book of Amos*, 10–20.

capital of an Assyrian province in 732. So a substantial core of the book must surely antedate 732.

Though the book of Amos now contains traces of hope, especially in the epilogue, its general tenor is of unremitting judgment, and this theme has survived all that later editors could do to tone down the message. Postexilic prophecy did not have this theme at its core but was concerned with the restoration and rejuvenation of the people of Judah (Yehud). While judgment followed by salvation is the pattern that has been imposed on earlier prophetic collections by postexilic editors, and that includes the editors of Amos, in the case of this book, the work has been accomplished only rather superficially, leaving a clear impression of a prophet of doom for whom there are very few glimmers of light. No one after the exile would have invented such a prophet.

Still further, the criticism of the cult, which in itself seems to indicate a time before the postexilic community came to center its life on the worship of the Temple, also contains preexilic features. It is directed against worship at Bethel and Gilgal, not Jerusalem, and it may include features of the cult that did not exist in postexilic times.[38]

Above all, perhaps, the general hypothesis that all the literature in the Old Testament that claims to come from the preexilic period is in fact the product of the postexilic community in Yehud strains

---

[38] See Hadjiev, *The Composition and Redaction of the Book of Amos*, 14–15: "the command to bring the tithe on the third day (4:4) presupposes an otherwise unattested custom of worshippers staying for three days at the sanctuary and bringing a sacrifice on the morning after arrival and the tithes on the third day. The command 'burn thank offering from leaven' (4:5) is contrary to the provision of Lev. 2:11 (cf. also Lev. 6:10 [17]; Ex. 23:18) and probably also reflects preexilic cultic practice." H. G. M. Williamson, "In Search of the Pre-exilic Isaiah," in *In Search of Pre-exilic Israel* (ed. J. Day; JSOTSup 406; London: T & T Clark, 2004), 181–206, argues that 5:21–22 also reflects preexilic practices.

credulity.[39] While it is in my judgment very unlikely that everything in the book of Amos comes from the eighth century, the
very discrepancies that lead us to think of later redactors are a sign
that there is material in the book that resists being assigned to the
postexilic period during which at least some of the book's redactors worked. In a word, the book is uneven, and that unevenness
results from the fact that material that took its origin in one set of
circumstances is being (re)applied in a later age. Both original and
later circumstances shine through the text, and this precludes our
attributing it all to only the later period(s) in which it was edited.

AMOS AND THE BOOK OF THE TWELVE

In Jewish tradition, the so-called Minor Prophets of the Hebrew
Bible are referred to as "the Book of the Twelve," and in recent
years there has been a movement that favors reading this unit
as a single book, rather like each of the Major Prophets Isaiah,
Jeremiah, and Ezekiel. Linked with this idea has been the suggestion that the twelve books may have been edited to form a single
whole, with some passages therefore added to each book not as
part of the redaction of the book itself, but at the moment when it
was incorporated into the Twelve. This was anticipated by Rolland
Emerson Wolfe in 1935,[40] but it was not until the 1990s that it began
to be developed in detail. James Nogalski proposed that there was
an early edition of four prophetic books, Hosea, Amos, Micah, and
Zephaniah, but the only "canonizing" additions he identified in
Amos belonged to the next stage, when Obadiah and Joel were

---

[39] For other arguments in favor of this, see John Day, ed., *In Search of Pre-exilic
Israel* (JSOTSup 406; London: T & T Clark, 2004).

[40] Rolland Emerson Wolfe, "The Editing of the Book of the Twelve," *ZAW* 53
(1935): 90–128.

also incorporated.[41] Amos 9:12a ("in order that they may possess the remnant of Edom") linked Amos with Obadiah, which is a prophecy against the Edomites, and 9:13 made a link with Joel. Subsequent work by Aaron Schart and Jakob Wöhrle, of which the latter is perhaps the most carefully worked out, has examined further the development of the Twelve.[42] Schart advocates a hypothesis about the growth of Amos as a whole, which is akin to the theories already examined. He thinks of six stages in the book's growth: the core of chapters 3–6, the original text of Amos, was augmented through the addition of the oracles against the nations and the visions to make an early edition of the whole book. At this point, Hosea was added to Amos to make a scroll of two prophets. Next came the deuteronomistic edition, which added Micah and Zephaniah, just as in Nogalski's model; then the "doxologies" were added, and at the same time Nahum and Habakkuk were reworked and added in. The two final stages involved first the addition of Haggai and Zechariah and then Joel and Obadiah. It was only then that Amos 9:11–15 came in to complete the book. Despite differences in detail from Nogalski, the process is conceptualized in a similar way: to begin with, the book of Amos itself is gradually redacted, but then it starts to be part of a growing collection and various passages and glosses are added to make it fit with the message(s) of the other prophetic books.

Wöhrle's more recent work has produced a similar scheme, which again thinks in terms of several early editions of the words

[41] See James Nogalski, *Literary Precursors to the Book of the Twelve* (BZAW 217; Berlin: Walter de Gruyter, 1993).

[42] Aaron Schart, *Die Entstehung des Zwölfprophetenbuchs: Neubearbeitungen von Amos im Rahmen schriftenübergreifender Redaktionsprozesse* (BZAW 260; Berlin: Walter de Gruyter, 1998); Jakob Wöhrle, *Die frühen Sammlungen des Zwölfprophetenbuches: Entstehung und Komposition* (BZAW 360; Berlin: Walter de Gruyter, 2006).

of Amos and then a gradual incorporation into larger collections until the Book of the Twelve is complete. He too sees parts of chapters 3–6 as the core of Amos, supplemented already in the eighth century by the addition of 3:3–6, 3:8, 5:6, and 5:14–15. Then, in the late preexilic period, the material critical of the cult was added, together with the oracles against the nations and the visions. By this time, there was thus a book of Amos with the main themes we still find in it already clearly recognizable: in essence, that is, the book is a preexilic composition. During the exile, the "doxologies" were added, but – and in this, Wöhrle challenges the emerging consensus – there was no combination with other prophetic books until the deuteronomistic redaction, which combined Amos (now augmented with the story in 7:10–17 and the oracles in 8:11–12 and 9:7–10) with Hosea, Micah, and Zephaniah. There were subsequent additions to Amos, for example 9:13 and 9:14–15, which correlated with the addition of other prophetic books, such as the combined collection Haggai-Zechariah.

Importantly, Wöhrle sees his work not merely as an exercise in the history of the composition of the prophetic books, but as a contribution to their interpretation. The "Book of the Four" (Hosea, Amos, Micah, Zephaniah) presented an interpretation of the history of Israel that sought to explain the events of the exile and the poor socioeconomic conditions of life under the Persians by tracing divine judgment back to various social and religious sins of the people in preexilic times. It also tried to show that the future lay with a remnant, the loyal poor who had been oppressed by the aristocracy in earlier days, but who would now form the core of a new Israel/Judah. These four prophetic books, unlike Deutero-Isaiah, do not envision the return of the exiles, but rather the reestablishment of those who had remained in the land as the essence of a renewed nation. Once again, we see here that critical questions about the origins and development of a prophetic book such as Amos cannot be separated from larger interpretative issues about the theology current at various periods and among various groups in the life of ancient Israel.

Not all scholars have been convinced that elements in the book of Amos came in at the stage of a redaction involving other books within the Twelve. Certainly, there are clear overlaps. Amos 1:2, for example, is almost identical with Joel 3:16 (Heb 4:16):

> The LORD roars from Zion,
>> and utters his voice from Jerusalem;
> the pastures of the shepherds wither,
>> and the top of Carmel dries up.

It is of course conceivable that this oracle was added to both books at the same time (though why this should be so is unclear); it is equally possible, however, and perhaps more likely, that one book borrowed it from the other, as with Micah 4:1–4 and Isaiah 2:2–5. If there was a stage at which Joel actually ended at 3:16 (Heb 4:16) and Amos did not yet have the title in Amos 1:1, then one book would have blended into the other, rather as with 2 Chronicles and Ezra, where the last verses of 2 Chronicles are very similar to the first verses of Ezra (2 Chr 36:22–23 and Ezra 1:1–4). There is, however, no independent evidence that anyone in antiquity ever read Joel and Amos as a single book or as parts of a single book.

Amos 9:13 is also similar to Joel 3:18 (Heb 4:18), but the two passages are not close to each other in the present arrangement of the two prophetic books. Perhaps the juxtaposition of Joel and Amos in the Book of the Twelve is somehow connected with the overlaps, but it is not obvious that this is or must be so, nor does it explain why the order is Joel–Amos rather than Amos–Joel. In sum, the identification of later additions to the prophetic books as a product of the growth of the canonical Twelve is difficult to prove, as against theories of the internal redaction of each individual book.

In general, then, theories of the growth of the Twelve as a single book are not necessarily as strong as the effort expended on them might lead one to expect. Ehud Ben Zvi has mounted a comprehensive attack on such theories, arguing that there was little perception in antiquity of the Book of the Twelve as a unity analogous to the books of Isaiah or Jeremiah.[43] The Twelve appeared on a single scroll because their combined length amounted to something similar to one of the books of the Major Prophets, but there was no implication that they should be read as forming a unitary work. The books are not unified by claiming to go back to a single prophetic figure, and many are overtly dated, in their superscription, to different periods in the history of Israel. Once it has been decided that the books were codified by being joined and edited together, it is possible, as Wöhrle has shown, to discern passages that could have been added at that stage, but there is no compelling reason to believe in such codification in the first place. The very variant orders of the books in different manuscripts of the Hebrew Bible, and the quite distinct tradition in the Greek Bible, are not encouraging for the hypothesis that what we have represents a final "edition" of the Twelve.[44] Where the books of the prophets

---

[43] Ehud Ben Zvi, "Twelve Prophetic Books or 'The Twelve'? A Few Preliminary Considerations," in *Forming Prophetic Literature: Essays on Isaiah and the Twelve in Honor of John D. W. Watts* (eds. J. W. Watts and P. R. House; JSOTSup 235; Sheffield: Sheffield Academic Press, 1996), 125–156.

[44] For the Greek Bible, see H. B. Swete, *Introduction to the Old Testament in Greek* (repr. ed.; Peabody, MA: Hendrickson, 1989 [orig: 1900]), 197–230. There is a full discussion in Roger T. Beckwith, *The Old Testament Canon of the New Testament Church and its Background in Early Judaism* (Grand Rapids: Eerdmans, 1986). See also Marvin A. Sweeney, "Sequence and Interpretation

that come toward the end in most canonical orders are concerned, there is a long tradition supporting their juxtaposition – Haggai, Zechariah, and Malachi are always together. But for Amos, Hosea, Joel, and Obadiah, the order varies. For the thesis of a coherent redaction of these books to be falsifiable, and hence worthwhile, one would need to be convinced that equally strong evidence of redaction could not be found if they were in a different order, and I am not sure this is forthcoming: most of the parallels found would work even if the order were different.

To be sure, it is possible that the Twelve were *read* as a unity, in such a way that people saw coherence and order in them, even if they were not *redacted* in relation to each other as Wöhrle and others propose. Paul R. House has suggested interpretative possibilities if we take the Book of the Twelve as a meaningful whole, despite how it was redacted.[45] Indeed, it is doubtful whether even the Major Prophets were actually read as unitary works, in the modern sense of the word "work": they were not seen as finished literary products but as collections of sayings (which in origin is exactly what they probably were!).[46] Later rabbinic or Christian sources never say "as it is written in the Book of the Twelve" but "as it is written in Amos/Hosea/etc." or "as it is written in the

---

in the Book of the Twelve," in *Reading and Hearing the Book of the Twelve* (eds. James Nogalski and Marvin A. Sweeney; SBLSymS 15; Atlanta: Society of Biblical Literature, 2000), 49–64, esp. 52.

[45] Paul R. House, *The Unity of the Twelve* (JSOTSup 97; Sheffield: Sheffield Academic Press, 1990). See also John Barton, "The Canonical Meaning of the Book of the Twelve," in *After the Exile: Essays in Honour of Rex Mason* (eds. D. R. Reimer and J. Barton; Macon, GA: Mercer University Press, 1996), 59–73.

[46] For this point, see the classic arguments of Benajmin Sommer, "The Scroll of Isaiah as Jewish Scripture, or, Why Jews Don't Read Books," in *Society of Biblical Literature 1996 Seminar Papers* (Atlanta: Scholars Press, 1996), 225–244.

prophets." This does not rule out the possibility that some did see the Twelve as a unity, but there is not much reason to think that this was in fact the case. It remains true that people in postexilic times did tend to think that there was a unitary "prophetic" message shared by *all* the ancient prophets,[47] and this resulted in Amos being assimilated to other prophets with whom he may, in reality, have had little in common. For example, later generations certainly thought that he had proclaimed a message of deliverance and restoration after judgment, and Christians thought this included salvation for the Gentiles:

> James replied, "My brothers, listen to me. Simeon has related how God first looked favorably on the Gentiles, to take from among them a people for his name. This agrees with the words of the prophets, as it is written,
>
> After this I will return,
> and I will rebuild the dwelling of David, which has fallen;
>   from its ruins I will rebuild it, and I will set it up,
> so that all other peoples may seek the Lord –
>   even all the Gentiles over whom my name has
>   been called.
>   Thus says the Lord, who has been making these
>   things known from long ago." (Acts 15:13–18;
>   cf. Amos 9:11–13)

But this has little to do with Amos's place in the Book of the Twelve and is simply a feature of how the prophets in general were read in antiquity.

THE PROPHET AND THE BOOK

I have set out a number of possible points on a spectrum, reaching all the way from confidence that everything in the book of Amos

---

[47] Compare again my *Oracles of God*.

comes from the prophet to complete scepticism that anything does. The truth does not necessarily lie equidistant from the two extremes, but my own judgment is that neither extreme is tenable. No one writing freely would have produced exactly the book of Amos as we now have it, and this point operates equally against both ends of the spectrum: it is equally unlikely that (a) the prophet himself would have presented his thoughts in the form now observable in the book, in which it is hard to find a great deal of overall coherence (despite some well-ordered sections), and (b) a writer of prophetic fiction in postexilic Yehud would have done so. The book is manifestly composite, and the oracles in it do not come from the same period. To take the limiting cases, 6:11–14 makes sense only in the light of recent Israelite victories against Aram and before both a devastating earthquake and a military invasion; 9:11–15 makes sense only if the Davidic dynasty has fallen in Judah and better times are awaited. The two passages cannot be from the same time. Furthermore, parts of the book are carefully patterned – the ring composition in the middle of chapters 3–6 is an example – while others look haphazard and seem to betray several hands. So the truth lies somewhere between the extreme ends of the compositional debate; but where?

With Hadjiev, I believe that there is extensive material in the book that requires a date in the mid-eighth century, which is not all that long after the period in which Amos is supposed to have lived and worked. This must raise the possibility that there are oracles in the book that genuinely go back to him, though authenticity can never be absolutely proven (nor disproven!). The quest for the historical Amos is like the quest for the historical Jesus in that most scholars think some sayings attributed to the person in question are likely to be genuine, yet in no case can it be definitively demonstrated. The "principle of dissimilarity" in Gospel criticism – roughly, the principle that a saying is authentic if no one would have made it up – can also be deployed in the study of the Old Testament, as can what Gerd Theissen and Dagmar Winter call the "principle of plausibility," where a saying is clearly thinkable in the circumstances of the person alleged to have uttered it.[48] Amos's strictures on the northern kingdom in many cases qualify under both principles: they fit plausibly in the middle of the eighth century, when we know from archaeological as well as textual evidence that the country was enjoying reasonable prosperity and had repelled the Arameans; and they are unlikely to have been invented by later generations, who thought of the prophets, as Ben Sira was to put it, as those "who comforted the people of Jacob and delivered them with confident hope" (Sir 49:10). Applying such principles as these moves us, I would argue, nearer to the conservative than to the radical end of the compositional debate, encouraging us to think that we can sometimes hear the authentic words of Amos. His message is so distinctive and in many ways so unattractive that it is unlikely to be simply fictitious.

At the same time, evidence of redaction and addition is obvious even to the naked eye, and some theory of multiple editions seems essential if all of the book is to be accounted for. Of recent theories, Hadjiev's is to me the most sober and probably the most plausible, though complete certainty is unattainable, and the more detailed the analysis becomes, the less certain it looks. Even so, despite the diversity of theories presently available, there are some points of convergence. Most scholars agree that a core of chapters 3–6 is early, and also that the oracles on the nations (or at least

---

[48] See Gerd Theissen and Dagmar Winter, *The Quest of the Plausible Jesus: The Question of Criteria* (trans. M. E. Boring; Louisville: Westminster John Knox, 2002).

the core five) and the five visions go back to an early collection and could be by Amos himself. In between, there may have been several reworkings; at this point matters are more speculative. At some point, a Judean perspective was introduced to the book, but that could be in the seventh century (as in Wolff's Josianic redaction) or later. Most critics think that there was a deuteronomistic redaction during the exilic age, which introduced the oracle against Judah (2:4–5) and tried to make Amos's message apply to the circumstances of the exile. The epilogue, as always, strikes most readers as an artificial hopeful addition to a book otherwise bathed in gloom, and the majority of critics attribute it to a postexilic editor. At that point, perhaps we really are dealing with someone who edited several books among the Twelve, and wanted to impart a confident note to them all (to produce the collection as Ben Sira would later read it).

Whatever the case, the more complex the theories about these various redactions become, the less they can be substantiated and the more they represent idiosyncratic readings by individual scholars. In the present study, I will not assume any detailed reconstruction of individual sections, but will work with three broad categories: (1) material that is reasonably likely to go back to the prophet or his first disciples; (2) material that must be from a later revision or redaction; and (3) material that seems to belong to the stage at which the book was completed, such as the superscription. I will not try to apportion the "secondary" oracles to exact dates, though I will note whether they seem to presuppose a preexilic, exilic, or postexilic ("Second Temple period") setting where this can reasonably be posited.

If we take it that an early core of the book, consisting of the oldest portions of the oracles against the nations in chapters 1–2, the "words" of chapters 3–6, and the vision reports in chapters 7–9, derives from either Amos himself or his disciples – and I myself do not think there is any way of distinguishing between the prophet himself and his early collectors – then the following passages seem to be redactional and so need to be assessed as part of the growth of the book from its earliest collection(s) into a finished whole:

1. *Amos 1:1* is the superscription to the whole book, and probably derives from the stage at which the book was incorporated into the collection of the Twelve. It is similar to the headings of a number of other prophetic books (e.g., Isa 1:1; Jer 1:1–3; Joel 1:1; Micah 1:1; Hab 1:1; Zeph 1:1).

2. *Amos 1:2* presumably comes from a Judean edition of the book, since it refers to Zion. It is worth remembering, however, that Amos was a Judean himself, and he could have regarded Zion as Yhwh's dwelling place, though there is no evidence for that anywhere else in the book. There is also the question of how this verse is related to Joel 3:14 (Heb 4:14). I am inclined to think that the editor of Joel borrowed it from Amos, but it is again possible that its occurrence in both books has something to do with their being placed together in the canon of the twelve minor prophets, as discussed earlier.

3. *Amos 1:9–12* contain oracles against Tyre and Edom. It has been usual for commentators to regard these oracles as a later addition to the original oracles against the nations on the basis that they are historically anomalous in the eighth century.[49] Edom in particular was not at all an enemy of Israel in the time of Amos, but became so when it sided with the Babylonians at the time of the exile. Note Obadiah 10–11 on this point:

---

[49] Compare my discussion in John Barton, *Amos's Oracles against the Nations* (SOTSMS 6; Cambridge: Cambridge University Press, 1980); reprinted in idem, *Understanding Old Testament Ethics* (Louisville: Westminster John Knox, 2003).

For the slaughter and violence done to your brother Jacob,
    shame shall cover you,
    and you shall be cut off for ever.
On the day that you stood aside,
    on the day that strangers carried off his wealth,
and foreigners entered his gates
    and cast lots for Jerusalem,
    you too were like one of them.

Anti-Edom material in the Old Testament generally comes from the exilic or postexilic period (cf. Mal 1:2–5). As for Tyre, the oracle seems to be more or less a copy of the Edom oracle, and, like it, is stylistically different from the other oracles against the nations. It is also hard to find any circumstances in Amos's lifetime to which it might refer.[50] With these two oracles (and that against Judah, see below) removed, we are left with five oracles against the nations balancing the five visions in chapters 7–9, arranged around the words of Amos in chapters 3–6. It is impossible to know if the earliest collection of Amos material had such an aesthetically satisfying shape, but it is an attractive hypothesis.

4. *Amos 2:4–5*, the oracle against Judah, has long been regarded as secondary. It somewhat spoils the dramatic effect of the oracles if they are designed to build up to a climax in the oracle against Israel,[51] at least if the hearers would have regarded Judah as part of "Israel," meaning the chosen people. But chiefly the Judah oracle stands out because it is so different in content from the other oracles. It does not deal with war crimes, as do the other foreign nation oracles, or with social injustices, as does the oracle against Israel, but rather concentrates on Judah's transgression of the law

---

[50] See my discussion in *Amos's Oracles against the Nations*, and the commentaries on the oracles in question.
[51] See Chapter 2 herein.

and (probably) its worship of other gods (the likely meaning of
"lies" here). The general consensus is that it belongs to the deuteronomistic redaction of Amos postulated by Schmidt, though not
all agree that it is deuteronomistic – Hayes, for example, points out
that the phraseology here is not actually found in deuteronomistic
texts, however much the ideas are.[52] But whether deuteronomistic
or not, it is surely the odd man out in its oracular context. Another
question arises: Is Amos likely to have attacked the southern
kingdom? We cannot tell – he must have known as much about
the South as about the North, indeed perhaps even more, since
he came from Tekoa.[53] But if he did intend to attack his fellow
Judeans, it is possible that he would have seen them as included in
the oracles against "Israel," taking that name to stand for the whole
people of YHWH rather than simply for the North. If so, a redactor, misunderstanding this and noticing that there was no explicit
condemnation of Judah in the book, might have added a specific
"Judah" oracle. The oracle fits very well into a period, subsequent
to Jeremiah, in which the prophets are seen as having taught the
law of Moses, and polemicized against breaches of it, rather than
the eighth century in which, as we will see, this was not the main
prophetic concern.

[52] Hayes, *Amos*, 101–104.
[53] It is sometimes suggested that Amos came from a northern town also called
Tekoa. See H. Schmidt, "Die Herkunft des Propheten Amos," in *Beiträge zur
alttestamentlichen Wissenschaft: Karl Budde zum siebzigsten Geburtstag am
13. April 1920 überreicht von Freunden und Schülern* (ed. Karl Marti; BZAW
34; Giessen: A. Töpelmann, 1920), 158–171. Jeremias argues strongly against
this: "His vocation as livestock breeder becomes especially comprehensible
here [i.e., in the Tekoa in Judah] and above all it best explains the striking differences between his proclamation and that of Hosea. Not least for this reason,
the search for a locale with the name Tekoa in the Northern Kingdom, a search
repeatedly undertaken from rabbinic exegesis up to the present, is futile from
the very outset" (*Amos*, 13; see also p. 2).

5. *Amos 3:7*, "Surely the Lord GOD does nothing without revealing his secret to his servants the prophets," is odd. The passage in which it appears, 3:3–8, has as its theme the necessity of prophesying once God has spoken. In a way, it is almost a "call narrative" for Amos, explaining that it is possible from effects to work back to causes. If two people are walking together, they must have agreed to meet; if a lion roars, it is because it has found prey; if a bird falls to the ground, it is because there is a trap; and so on. These examples from the natural world then lead up to the point that if Amos is prophesying, it must be because God has sent him. His prophecy is not fortuitous or random, but reflects a divine purpose. Verse 7 interrupts the flow of this argument with a general statement (possibly in prose) that works in the opposite direction: nothing happens unless it has been foretold. Furthermore, the foretelling happens through "his servants the prophets," which is a characteristically deuteronomistic expression. It sets Amos in a line of descent, as part of a prophetic institution, which seems at least on the face of it to be at variance with 7:14, where Amos is presented as denying that he is a prophet in the technical sense. Most commentators therefore regard v. 7 as a redactional addition, probably from the same stratum as the oracle against Judah. It belongs to a time when the prophets are seen as forming an institutional line going back to Moses. Its underlying conception is that God never acts unexpectedly, but always gives warning through his prophets. If Amos is seen primarily as a prophet of repentance, then this picture can be applied to him to some extent, but if (as I will argue) he is best painted in darker colors, then the "helpfulness" of prophecy that is here asserted would not comfortably apply to him.

6. We come to the question of the three "doxologies" found in *Amos 4:13*; *5:8–9*; and *9:5–6*. Most commentators have seen these as an important part of the book, and they have a dark quality that is

compatible with his way of seeing things.[54] On the other hand, they do not appear to be part of any of the passages within which they stand, but look like later insertions. This is even more the case if, as some think, they are originally three stanzas of a single hymn in praise of YHWH as creator and destroyer. We then have to explain why the hymn was pulled apart in this way, and it is possible that the placement of the three texts is in some way strategic, though attempts to explain the arrangment have not generally been very convincing. But from the point of view of the history of the book's composition, it would at any rate be right to say that they do not derive from Amos or his immediate circle but came in at a later stage. They are theologically very rich, and I will devote time to them later in this study.

7. *Amos 5:25*, "Did you bring to me sacrifices and offerings the forty years in the wilderness, O house of Israel?" is by general consent written in prose, which already makes it suspect, since Amos otherwise communicates in verse. It is quite in keeping with Amos's attacks on the cult as displeasing to YHWH, since it is a question clearly expecting the answer "no": Israel did not offer sacrifice during the wilderness period. The logic of the argument is that sacrifice is therefore not part of YHWH's wish for Israel. Jeremiah develops the same point later (see Jer 7:22). The wilderness is here regarded as the time when Israel did what was right, as in Hosea 2:13; 9:10; and Jeremiah 2:2–3. It is not impossible that Amos espoused this belief, which is also implicitly found in Deuteronomy – since the deuteronomic legislation about sacrifice is meant to apply once Israel gets into the Promised Land and therefore, presumably, it

---

[54] On the "negative theology" of the "doxologies," see Susan E. Gillingham, "'Der die Morgenröte zur Finsternis macht': Gott und Schöpfung im Amosbuch," *EvT* 53 (1993): 109–123.

did not apply during the wilderness wanderings. But most scholars have seen the verse as a development of Amos's message rather than as an original part of it, a prose gloss on Amos's condemnation of sacrifice. This seems to me difficult to decide: in my judgment, the verse could go back to Amos or his circle.

8. *Amos 5:26–27* is a prophecy of the Exile, and this is presented as a punishment for the worship of two deities, Sakkuth and Kaiwan, who are not mentioned elsewhere in the Old Testament.[55] In general, Amos appears to have condemned the wrong worship *of* YHWH – worshipping him through sacrifice rather than through correct behavior toward other people – and not the worship of other gods, as here. Further, the idea that the gods are "images that you made for yourselves" echoes the Isaianic and, especially, Deutero-Isaianic treatment of other gods as the work of human hands (see Isa 2:8; 46:6–7). It is thus unlikely that the verses derive from Amos or his immediate disciples. They seem instead to belong to a stage in the book's growth when Amos is seen, like the other prophets, as the scourge of "idolatry." Note that these verses, too, are in prose.

9. *Amos 7:10–15* is problematic in its present location because it interrupts the series of five visions. As a narrative account of Amos's encounter with the priest Amaziah at Bethel, it is in prose, and it speaks of Amos in the third person, which means presumably that it comes at best from disciples of the prophet and not from his own hand (unless, like Julius Caesar, Amos spoke of himself in this way). But a majority of commentators think that, though it may be misplaced in its present position, it does reflect a real memory of the prophet. The fact that he denies that he is a *nābî'* ("prophet")

---

55 Kaiwan is probably Saturn. See John Day, *Yahweh and the Gods and Goddesses of Canaan* (JSOTSup 265; New York: Continuum, 2002), 222.

is striking enough, for in later times he was certainly regarded as one, and it seems unlikely that redactors would have invented such a tradition. I will therefore treat this passage as giving us genuine information about Amos, even though it disrupts the symmetry of what we are seeing as the earliest structure of the book.

10. Most of *chapter 8* breaks the orderly progression of the vision reports, though that does not in itself imply that the material does not come from Amos or his immediate circle. Amos 8:4–6 seems to be a summary of 2:6–8, and looks almost like an alternative version of Amos's words there, but it may equally well be another oracle by the prophet on the same theme. From v. 7 onwards, we seem to have several oracles on the coming destruction. On the principle that later editors toned down Amos's message of doom rather than augmented it, we would have to think that these too are possibly authentic sayings. But vv. 11–12, with their much more general prediction of a time when "the word of the LORD" will become inaccessible and there will be a "famine ... of hearing the words of the LORD," does not fit with the rest of Amos's message, which otherwise seems to be concerned with *literal* famine, not a metaphorical one (a failure in divine communication). It is difficult, however, to think of a suitable setting for the oracle in any other period, unless it reflects a postexilic belief in the demise of prophecy. Verses 13–14 are untypical of Amos in being concerned with the worship of gods other than YHWH, but since they mention gods worshipped in Samaria and Dan, they fit better in the eighth century than in any other period. In sum, then, it is possible that much of chapter 8 consists of oracles that are genuinely early but have only a loose connection with Amos, or are augmentations of his oracles by fairly early disciples.

11. *Amos 9:8b*, "except that I will not utterly destroy the house of Jacob, says the LORD," looks like an addition designed to mitigate

the harshness of the preceding oracle ("The eyes of the Lord GOD are upon the sinful kingdom, and I will destroy it from the face of the earth"), and surely cries out that it was inserted at a later stage of redaction. It is not unlike Jeremiah 4:27:

> For thus says the LORD: The whole land shall be a desolation;
> yet I will not make a full end.

It is a reflection after the event, probably after the exile, by someone who wished to make the prediction conform to the reality that there was a "remnant" of Israel left as the nucleus of a new nation. Amos 9:8a is a thoroughgoing oracle of destruction on the sinful kingdom, and the addition of v. 8b certainly spoils its dramatic effect.

12. *Amos 9:9–10* is difficult to evaluate:

> For lo, I will command,
>> and shake the house of Israel among all the nations
> as one shakes with a sieve,
>> But no pebble shall fall to the ground.
> All the sinners of my people shall die by the sword,
>> who say, "Evil shall not overtake or meet us."

The image of sieving tends to imply that good and bad within the nation are being separated out, which is not wholly in keeping with Amos's general message that *everyone* comes under divine judgment, good and bad alike. It fits better with the ideas of postexilic prophetic texts that the judgment of God discriminates between the righteous and the wicked (cf. Zeph 3:11–13) – an idea we first encounter in Ezekiel 9:3–6. At the very least, the usual reconstruction of how prophetic thinking on this subject developed works with some such model: Amos, Hosea, and Isaiah thought in terms of an indiscriminate judgment, whereas Jeremiah and Ezekiel began to speculate about the salvation of the righteous in the general collapse of the nation, and still later prophets believed that the righteous would form the core of a new Israel. The problem is that this picture rests on a decision to regard passages such as Amos 9:9–10 as secondary – in other words, there is a danger of circularity in the argument. But the message of Amos seems to me so uncompromisingly negative that I regard the reconstruction as reasonable, though it cannot by any means be proven.

13. *Amos 9:11–12* is the first part of what is often referred to as the "epilogue" to Amos, and the idea that it is an addition to the book is one of the oldest and most well-established conclusions in the study of the prophetic book. The oracle's implication that the line of David has ended is generally agreed to place it during or after the Exile, as does the reference to the renewed people (presumably the people of Judah) possessing the "remnant of Edom." Edom had not fallen to any enemy in the days of Amos, and, as mentioned earlier, Israelite animus against Edom seems to derive from the collaboration of Edomites with the Babylonians at the sack of Jerusalem. A prophecy of what amounts to a Davidic empire ("Edom and all the nations who are called by my name," or "over whom my name is called" – that is, who are my possession) seems hardly likely in the mouth of Amos or his immediate circle. Whether this should be called "deuteronomistic" is less certain, however. The expression "booth of David" does not appear anywhere else in the Old Testament and so is not a marker of deuteronomistic authorship. But that the verses belong to a later stratum in the book seems reasonably certain.

14. Finally, *Amos 9:13–15* (which has some relation to Joel 3:18) prophesies miraculous fruitfulness in the renewed land, with harvests so plentiful that they cannot be fully gathered before it is time to plant the next. It belongs to a host of postexilic prophecies of fruitfulness (Isa 11:1–9; 65:17–25; Hag 2:18–19; Zech 8:11–13), and

looks forward to a restoration that will never again be followed by destruction or desolation. Its effect is to make Amos a prophet of salvation, like all the prophets in their final form. Hayes has defended its authenticity:

> In no way does it deny the coming disaster. The passage shows no special pro-Jerusalem or pro-Davidic claims. The text makes no reference to a return from exile, to divine forgiveness, or to the role of a Messianic figure, as one might expect, had the text originated in late exilic or postexilic times.[56]

But it seems to me that the widespread consensus treating the passage as secondary is more likely to be correct: we are here in a different world from the world of Amos. I therefore treat it as part of the final edition of the book.

The preceding discussion indicates that my proposals amount to a relatively conservative assessment of what is original and what is secondary in the book of Amos. They make it possible and sensible to devote a chapter to the theology of Amos and his disciples, and not only to that of the book in its finished form. Whatever one may think about the "authority" of the finished form, mere intellectual curiosity should make us take an interest in the teaching of the prophet himself if we think there is a realistic prospect of reconstructing it.

---

[56] Hayes, *Amos*, 228.

CHAPTER 2

Religious Belief and Practice in Amos's Day

Amos was Israel's first theologian. As far as we know, no one before him had subjected the religious beliefs and practices of people in Israel to critical scrutiny. His message was delivered in short, pithy sayings, but they were soon collected into larger complexes: I have suggested that not too long after his prophetic activity there existed three collections: the oracles against the nations (now found in chapters 1–2), an anthology of sayings (chapters 3–6), and a cycle of visions (chapters 7–9). In these, we encounter a strikingly original figure, with an uncompromising message of impending doom justified by a moral analysis of society and of the wider political world, even on an international scale.

According to 7:14, Amos was an agriculturalist, probably a sheep breeder rather than a simple shepherd. From the oracles preserved in the book, we can see that he had an education. This is apparent not only from the fact that he was able to produce oracles in well-formed Hebrew verse, but also because he sometimes used types of sayings that are really at home in the non-prophetic sphere, such as the funeral lament (5:1–2) and the numerical proverb (1:3). If he did not write himself – and there is no way of knowing whether he did or not – then he had literate disciples who were able to compile his sayings into coherent collections and to produce the core of the present book as an orderly whole. Evidence that his oracles were known to Isaiah later in the eighth century[1] suggests that written transmission ensured that his oracles became known outside the immediate circle of his followers.

Amos's theology was formed, as theology nearly always is, in dialogue with and in opposition to various popular beliefs and practices. To analyze his own teaching, we therefore need to have some knowledge of what was generally believed in his day – just as to understand Martin Luther, say, we need to know something about the religious belief system of late-medieval Europe. The complicating factor in the case of Amos is that the book of Amos itself constitutes much of the evidence for what was in fact believed in eighth-century Israel, so there is a danger of circularity. Sometimes we can supplement what we reconstruct of the religious world of Israel in this period from the evidence of other books, such as Hosea and Isaiah, and from archaeological discoveries in the region. But for the most part, we are dependent on Amos himself. He does, however, often visibly enter into dialogue with his contemporaries, and we can often argue that his message would not have made sense to them or would not have had the cutting edge it evidently had unless they had believed or done certain things. Short as the eighth-century core of the book is, it nevertheless provides quite a lot of insight into the beliefs and practices of the people of the time.

POPULAR IDEAS OF GOD

Amos's message makes no sense unless his contemporaries in Israel held certain beliefs about their god, Yhwh. As Julius Wellhausen

---

[1] As argued first in modern times by Reinhard Fey, *Amos und Jesaja: Abhängigkeit und Eigenständigkeit des Jesaja* (WMANT 12; Neukirchen-Vluyn: Neukirchener Verlag, 1963).

observed in the late nineteenth century, the belief of Israel before the advent of the great prophets appears to have been that "Yhwh is the God of Israel, and Israel is the people of Yhwh." In other words, there was thought to be a natural, self-evident bond between Israel and its god – as Wellhausen strikingly put it, the word "god" was more or less synonymous with "helper."[2] Yhwh was the god who was in a relationship of mutual commitment to Israel, and people at large had no special theory about how the relationship worked: ideas such as "covenant" or "election" were, as we will see, later theological interpretations of what was felt to be a purely natural relationship. Amos bears witness that the people believed Yhwh had brought them from Egypt into the Promised Land:

> You only have I known
> of all the families of the earth. (Amos 3:2a)

This suggests that the story of Moses and the exodus was known in some form. It indicated that Yhwh stood by Israel in times of affliction, and, like all national gods in the ancient Near East, Yhwh was the protector of his people in battle. There was absolutely no sense that the nation's relationship with Yhwh was conditional – as we will see, this idea is very much Amos's contribution to the theology of his time. Yhwh may thus be called the national god, just as Chemosh was the god of Moab or Qaus the god of Edom.

It is important to see, however, that Yhwh was not regarded as having only local scope, as if limited to the land of Israel and without power anywhere else. This is the impression we get from

---

[2]   Julius Wellhausen, *Prolegomena to the History of Ancient Israel with a Reprint of the Article Israel from the Encyclopaedia Britannica* (trans. J. S. Black and A. Menzies; repr. ed.; Cleveland: World Publishing, 1965), 469: "As for the substance of the national faith, it was summed up principally in the proposition that Jehovah is the God of Israel. But 'God' was equivalent to 'helper;' that was the meaning of the word. 'Help,' assistance in all occasions of life, – that was what Israel looked for from Jehovah, not 'salvation' in the theological sense."

the story of Elisha in 2 Kings 5, where the king of Aram is supposed to learn through the healing of Naaman that "there is no god except in Israel," and Naaman himself takes some Israelite soil back with him to Aram so that he can worship YHWH there (5:17). This presupposes that YHWH is indeed local, that is, limited to the land of Israel, and can be worshipped only if one is standing on the soil of the land. When Ezekiel sees the glory of YHWH leaving the Temple and preparing to fly off to Babylon (Ezek 10:18–22), we get the impression that, until this moment, YHWH has been understood as rooted in the Temple, so that the idea that he could go and take up his abode in another country – especially the country of the great enemy, Babylon! – is a novel and challenging one.

In Amos, however, it seems as though his audience must already have thought of YHWH as active outside the confines of Israel, since he was able to rescue them from the Egyptians. This must imply a belief in what we might call the ubiquity or perhaps the mobility of YHWH. Since Amos uses the assertion that Israel was brought from Egypt by YHWH as the basis on which to argue that they are therefore the object of his close attention – and will in fact be punished rather than rewarded – he must have assumed that people in Israel would have accepted as given the idea that YHWH's power did thus reach beyond the confines of the Promised Land. This is more than we would know from archaeological remains, which show clearly that the god YHWH was worshipped in eighth-century Israel but do not, given the nature of the evidence, help us to understand how YHWH was conceptualized.

The evidence is inconclusive and much debated, but it seems plausible that, in this period, YHWH may have had a consort, and hence that Israel was not in the later sense monotheistic.[3] Indeed,

---

[3] See William G. Dever, *Did God Have a Wife? Archaeology and Folk Religion in Ancient Israel* (Grand Rapids: Eerdmans, 2005).

we know from the Old Testament itself that many gods were worshipped in Israel right through the years of the monarchy, and that there was some kind of pantheon in which YHWH may or may not have been the chief god (see, for example, Psalm 82, which seems to attest to belief in a "council of the gods" in Israel). So we cannot speak of widespread monotheism in Israel at this time. From Hosea, we learn that many Israelites worshipped Baal – which is strictly speaking a title ("lord") rather than a proper name for the leading Canaanite god – and it sounds as though many identified this god with YHWH:

> On that day, says the LORD, you will call me "My husband," and no longer will you call me, "My Baal." For I will remove the names of the Baals from her mouth, and they shall be mentioned by name no more. (Hos 2:16–17)

There can be little doubt that polytheism was the normal religion of Israel in practice.[4] Nevertheless, the beliefs Amos presupposes in his hearers include a scope for YHWH far greater than that of a purely "local" god, or of one god among many others, and thus they contain the seeds of later monotheism within them. The God of the exodus is a god who can move nations around on the face of the earth and is therefore a world ruler. This is apparent also from Amos 9:7:

> Did I not bring Israel up from the land of Egypt,
>   and the Philistines from Caphtor and the Aramaens from Kir?

---

[4] On popular religion in Israel see Francesca Stavrakopoulou, "'Popular' Religion and 'Official' Religion: Practice, Perception, Portrayal," in *Religious Diversity in Ancient Israel and Judah* (eds. F. Stavrakopoulou and J. Barton; London: T & T Clark, 2010), 37–58. This essay problematizes the distinction between popular and official religion, a distinction that was not necessarily obvious at the time to everyone, even though the Old Testament gives the impression that it was.

It is unlikely here that Amos is saying something that his hearers would have found novel or surprising at this point. His argument rests on acceptance of the premise that Yʜwʜ had indeed stood behind the movement of several peoples from their original homeland to their present location, in order to go on to draw the much less acceptable conclusion that this demotes Israel from its purportedly special position in Yʜwʜ's eyes.[5] The unpalatable conclusion does not work unless the premise is taken for granted.

THE ORACLES AGAINST THE NATIONS: MORALITY IN WAR

The international scope of Yʜwʜ is even more apparent in the oracles against the nations in the first two chapters of the book. To understand the theological implications of these chapters, we must first appreciate their rhetorical effect. The arrangement of the oracles is not random. True, we do not know for sure how a decision was made about the order of the foreign nations that are accused of war crimes. But it is clear that the culmination of the sequence in an oracle against Israel itself is a deliberate part of the structure. The audience has to be imagined applauding after each oracle against a foreign nation, beginning with Aram, which the Israelite army had only recently defeated in order to win back two towns in Transjordan (Amos 6:13). This is the kind of thing an audience would expect from a prophet. The oracle against Israel is thus meant to wipe the smile off their faces, as Yʜwʜ turns from judgment on their enemies to judgment on themselves.

---

[5]   See Walter Brueggemann, "'Exodus' in the Plural (Amos 9:7)," in *Many Voices, One God: Being Faithful in a Pluralistic World* (eds. Walter Brueggemann and George W. Stroup; Louisville: Westminster John Knox, 1998), 15–34, reprinted in idem, *Texts That Linger, Words That Explode* (ed. Patrick D. Miller; Minneapolis: Fortress, 2000), 89–103, 125–129.

This rhetorical effect implies quite a number of assumptions about the audience, which I have analyzed in my monograph *Amos's Oracles against the Nations.*[6] Most obviously, it implies that YHWH has the power to inflict disaster on nations other than his own. This is commonplace ancient Near Eastern theology, not in any way peculiar to Israel. Throughout the ancient world, a nation's god – especially, in the case of polytheistic systems, its god of war – is seen as the source of victory over the enemy. Even so, the oracles in Amos are interesting in implying that YHWH judges other nations *even when they are not at war with Israel,* and *even when the offense they have committed is not directed against Israel* because the crime of the Moabites in 2:1 is an atrocity perpetrated against the Edomites:

> Thus says the LORD:
> For three transgressions of Moab, and for four,
>   I will not revoke the punishment;
> because he burned to lime
>   the bones of the king of Edom.

It is possible to argue that the brotherhood between Israel and Edom, symbolized in the relation of Jacob and Esau in Genesis, meant that a crime against Edom was felt to be also in some way anti-Israelite, but this is not very plausible. It is more likely that YHWH was felt to have moral authority outside the borders of Israel. It is not certain in 1:6 that the crime of the Philistines in "carr[ying] into exile entire communities, to hand them over to Edom" is necessarily directed against Israelites – and note that, in this oracle, Edom is evidently seen as hostile, not as an ally. Thus

---

6   John Barton, *Amos's Oracles against the Nations* (SOTSMS 6; Cambridge: Cambridge University Press, 1980); reprinted in idem, *Understanding Old Testament Ethics* (Louisville: Westminster John Knox, 2003).

Yhwh has a moral authority that reaches beyond the bounds of his chosen people, and he is some kind of universal god – and this is true not only for Amos and his own circle, but also for the people he is addressing.

This must imply a belief in some kind of universal moral norms of conduct in war. There were conventions governing war in the ancient world – not of course internationally policed, as under our modern Geneva Convention, but simply part of the belief system of individual nations. In Israel, there were certainly ideas about what kind of conduct was acceptable in war, as we see from 2 Kings 6:22. Some scholars have argued that Amos is implying an acceptance by other nations of Israelite norms in these matters on the basis of some kind of treaty or agreement – perhaps there was even some sense that the nations condemned in chapters 1 and 2 had formed part of the Davidic "empire" and so had special mutual obligations to proper conduct. But the prophet speaks as though there was almost a kind of self-evidence about the moral norms contravened by the nations, as though they were conventions any right-minded person would recognize. Nor is there any statement that the norms derive from a God-given agreement such as the covenant. They seem instead to represent human conventions, but human conventions that God is seen to support with sanctions. It looks as if people in Israel had certain beliefs about what it was acceptable to do even in wartime, which they thought other nations ought to accept too. That would make ancient Israelite society very like many other societies, both ancient and modern, in which most people have a more or less vague sense that certain things are outrageous, and expect God or the gods to do something about them by way of payback or vengeance. Amos builds on this widespread social consensus, and dramatically exploits it to confront the people with their own (non-military) misconduct and suggest that it is as bad as, or even worse than, the atrocities committed by foreigners at war.

For this dramatic trick to work, it cannot have been normally believed that the kinds of social injustice committed in Israel were in any way on a par with atrocities in warfare. And that is surely what we would expect. It is genuinely surprising to suggest that exploiting the poor by sharp practice in commerce is culpable in the same way as torturing people to death when invading their country. Clearly, Amos's audience did not see matters in that way; neither would we expect them to have done so.

Would people have been surprised in general by the fact that Amos proclaimed judgment on the nations? Probably not. This was one of the functions of prophets in the ancient Near East: to reassure the ruler of their own nation (for prophets almost always spoke to kings) by declaring that the gods would wreak vengeance on the monarch's enemies. The "oracles against the nations" genre may indeed have already been fixed prior to Amos. It appears in other prophetic books (e.g., Isa 13–23; Ezek 25–32), though Amos of course provides the earliest example and could in principle be innovating. But texts such as the Egyptian execration texts show that forms like this did exist widely in the ancient world. What was certainly *not* expected was that the prophet should declare the god's judgment on his *own* nation. After the fact – in this case, an unfortunate outcome to some event such as a defeat in battle, for instance – kings might conclude that the god had been angry with his land, and therefore stirred up an enemy to destroy it, as Mesha of Moab alleged on the Moabite Stone dated to the ninth century BCE:

> As for Omri, king of Israel, he humbled Moab many days for Chemosh was angry at his land. And his son followed him and he

also said, "I will humble Moab." In my time he spoke [thus], but I have triumphed over him and over his house, while Israel has perished for ever.[7]

But before an event of some sort, to judge from ancient Mesopotamian parallels, prophets might at most warn that a defeat could be impending, but certainly not that the nation was to be completely overthrown. In saying the latter, Amos steps out of his role as a prophet, if indeed "prophet" is the right term to describe him at this juncture. It is clear not only from the external evidence but also from the internal logic of Amos's argument that his audience did not expect prophets to proclaim complete national disaster. The prophet's role was to be *helpful* to the nation, by warning of possible risks in military undertakings, as well as by promising divine blessings; it was *not* to *condemn* the nation, as though the prophet were the nation's very own enemy.

THE DAY OF YHWH

Thus from the oracles against the nations, we can deduce a good deal about popular belief in Amos's day about morality, warfare, and the role of prophets, which largely supports, so far as there is evidence, what is known from other sources. But other parts of Amos's teaching are also rich in evidence for what his audience believed. An example is 5:18–20:

> Alas for you who desire the day of the Lord!
>> Why do you want the day of the Lord?
> It is darkness, not light;
>> as if someone fled from a lion,
>> and was met by a bear;

---

[7] *ANET*, 320.

> or went into the house and rested a hand against the wall,
>   and was bitten by a snake.
> Is not the day of the LORD darkness,
>   not light,
> and gloom with no brightness in it?

It is clear from this text that there was a popular expectation in Amos's time of something called "the day of YHWH." In later times, this became a technical term for the day of divine judgment: we see this in Isaiah 2:12 and Zephaniah 1:14–18. (It is from these passages that the Christian expression for the Last Judgment, *dies irae* – the "day of wrath" – derives.) But a history of this term should proceed by examining what the background must have been, since Amos is able to refer to it as something people *already* know about and to which they are looking forward. If Amos condemns people in Northern Israel in his time who were looking forward to an occasion or event they referred to as "the day of YHWH," then this must have formed part of a widespread popular expectation – otherwise his condemnation would have made no sense to his hearers. Furthermore, we may be able to learn a little more about the character of this supposedly joyful "day" by seeing what kind of inversion of it Amos ironically instructs his audience to expect. If the day is to be "darkness, and not light," then presumably it was a "day" (not necessarily in the literal sense of a twenty-four hour period, but possibly in the broader sense of an "occasion") to which people looked for "light." "Light" here is probably a metaphor for success and prosperity. Since their experience on that "day" will be "as if someone fled from a lion and was met by a bear, or went into the house and rested a hand against the wall, and was bitten by a snake" (5:19), then the popular expectation must have been of something good or pleasant that would induce a relaxed and comfortable feeling – the very opposite of this experience of being driven from pillar to post by a succession of terrors. All in all, then, there must have been a popular expectation of a "day" on which God would bless his people and make them happy.

Disagreement begins, however, when scholars try to get a sharper focus on just what sort of occasion was envisioned.[8] There have been two main proposals. Sigmund Mowinckel argued that the "day" in question must be a cultic or liturgical occasion, a festival in fact.[9] This may be supported by noting that the passage continues immediately after Amos's denunciation of expectations of the day with "I hate, I despise your *festivals*, and I take no delight in your *solemn assembles*" (5:21) – though this observation assumes that this pericope was originally linked to 5:18–20 and has not been placed here editorially, as would probably be the majority view. The expectation of "light," in the cultic interpretation of the Old Testament that Mowinckel pioneered, would be a very natural one in the context of a cultic "day." Amos's announcement that, quite to the contrary, doom would fall on the day of Yнwн would thus be very much as if we were to think that some dreadful disaster was going to fall on Christmas Day. Indeed, when the terrible tsunami struck Southeast Asia on December 26, 2004, there was exactly this kind of sense that the suffering was compounded by its happening at just such a time of year. One point that may be urged in support of Mowinckel's position is that

---

[8] For what follows, see John Barton, "The Day of Yahweh in the Minor Prophets," in *Biblical and Near Eastern Essays: Studies in Honour of Kevin J. Cathcart* (JSOTSup 375; eds. C. McCarthy and J. F. Healy; London: T & T Clark, 2004), 68–79.

[9] Sigmund Mowinckel, "Tronstigningssalmerne og Jahwes tronstigningsfest," *Norsk theologi til reformasjonsjubileet* (Spesialhefte *NTT*; 1917): 13–79; idem, *Psalmenstudien* II (Kristiania: J. Dybwad, 1922); and, idem, *He That Cometh: The Messiah Concept in the Old Testament and Later Judaism* (trans. G. W. Anderson; Oxford: Blackwell, 1956).

the imminence of the "day" is not only asserted by Amos, but presupposed by him as part of the popular hope he is countering. If
he had in mind a specific coming festival, this would make excellent sense, for his hearers would actually know exactly when the
"day" was due to fall, and he could give his prophecy a particularly
strong claim by maintaining that it would be *on that very day* that
disaster would strike.

The other main explanation of the "day of YHWH" has been that
of Gerhard von Rad, who took the term to mean "the day of YHWH's
battle," deriving it from the (putative) Holy War tradition.[10] This
theory goes back still earlier to R. H. Charles.[11] Von Rad argued
that, like the "day of Midian" in Isaiah 9:4, the "day of YHWH" was
the name of a day when YHWH routed his enemies on the battle-
field and gave victory to Israel – or rather, the day on which he
would do so in the future. It was part of a popular hope, sometimes described as "popular eschatology." Amos saw that his
contemporaries, who were already at war with the Arameans and
were likely, in his view, soon to be oppressed by the Assyrians,
had a groundless assurance that YHWH would stand by them in
all their conflicts. In particular, there would come a day when he
would destroy not simply this or that enemy but all the foes of his
holy people, on a "day" he had appointed. On this interpretation,
Amos's audience was confidently looking forward to a reasonably
imminent implementation of this promise of help. Amos's task was

---

[10] Gerhard von Rad, "The Origin of the Concept of the Day of Yahweh," *JSS* 4
      (1959): 97–108.
[11] R. H. Charles, *A Critical History of the Doctrine of a Future Life in Israel, in
      Judaism, and in Christianity; or, Hebrew, Jewish, and Christian Eschatology
      from Pre-prophetic Times till the Close of the New Testament Canon: Being
      the First Jowett Lectures Delivered in 1898–99* (2nd ed.; London: A. & C. Black,
      1913).

to inform them that there would indeed be a "day of YHWH," but it would reverse all their confident expectations: the enemy would *overpower them* instead of being overpowered. But this would not spell the defeat of YHWH; on the contrary, YHWH himself would stand behind the enemy assault and guarantee its success.

There seems little hope of deciding between these two explanations of the day of YHWH in Amos. But it is worth emphasizing three points on which they agree:

1. First, there was a popular hope of divine intervention in world affairs, which would establish Israel in a position of supremacy vis-à-vis other nations, and especially its enemies. This was not a hope for some otherworldly realm, but for the transformation of the present world order into a situation much more favorable to Israel. It might be accompanied by great meteorological disturbances – earthquake, fire, and so on – but it was not to be a "cosmic" event that would change the course of nature itself or affect the order of the whole universe. Whether it was to be brought about by a unilateral act of YHWH on a cultically significant occasion, or by his cooperation with the armies of Israel in conflict with their enemies, it would greatly change the present state of political relations in the Syro-Palestinian area and perhaps in the whole ancient Near East.

2. The hope had a certain urgency to it: it was not a matter of an expectation about the very remote future, but rather a belief that *very soon* YHWH would step in to rectify the difficult condition of his people. This is clearly relevant to Amos's own assertion that the day of YHWH is indeed coming soon, even though its character will be the exact opposite of what people are expecting.

3. In keeping with what was argued above in the case of the oracles against the nations, such a hope would not have been possible unless people in general believed that YHWH's power extended

beyond Israel and controlled the other nations – a belief that was normal in the ancient Near East where most nations attributed victory over foreigners to their own god or gods. YHWH's universal dominion was the presupposition of popular hope, not an idea first conjured up by the prophets. Amos is not being original in asserting that YHWH controls the fates of all nations in Israel's general area; his originality comes in claiming that YHWH will exercise this control *against*, rather than *for*, the interests of Israel, his own special people. That is the scandal of Amos's message.

SACRIFICE AND TEMPLES

Another general assumption that Amos's hearers must have held – and indeed, we know that more or less everyone in the ancient Near East held the same – was that divine beings required sacrifice from mortals. YHWH, like any other god worshipped in the region, expected his worshippers to offer animals and vegetable crops in sacrifice. In so far as the relationship of the nation and its god was conditional at all, the condition was the regular offerings at the sanctuaries. It is clear from Amos's teaching that the people among whom he functioned made pilgrimages to various shrines, Bethel and Gilgal in particular (3:4–5), where they brought their sacrifices. Amos apparently disapproved of the sacrificial cult, but it is evident that the people he was speaking to took it for granted that sacrifice was pleasing to YHWH. The impression his prophecy leaves us with is that they did not think YHWH was interested in anything else, and though this may be a tendentious reading of the situation on Amos's part, it comports reasonably well with ancient attitudes to the gods in general. The maintenance of good relations between gods and humans largely depended, in the ancient world, on the maintenance of the system of sacrificial offerings. Certainly, at the national level, the prosperity of the nation depended on continuing to enjoy the favor of the gods, and for that, the national institutions, primarily the temples and shrines, needed to keep up a steady supply of sacrifices. There was no idea in the ancient world that the gods could be satisfied with the nation if it failed to make the appointed offerings. Here, Amos's message was extremely radical.

The role of the prophet was also related to the life of sanctuaries, since it was in the context of a particular shrine that a prophet functioned, and the impression given by 7:10–17 is that the priest of Bethel, Amaziah, believed Amos to be under his jurisdiction, which may indicate that this was the general relationship between priests and prophets. There is plenty of comparative evidence showing that, in the ancient Near East, the cult center was often the place where prophetic activity was manifested – there, and the royal court.[12] It was in the cult center that the prophet was expected to exercise his skill in commenting on national military policy. It seems as if Amos ran true to this expectation in speaking at the shrine in Bethel, but that he systematically defeated it in speaking against the interests of the nation instead of serving them.

MORALITY

I said above that Amos's audience does not seem to have thought that the relationship between the nation and YHWH depended on anything except sacrifice. This does not imply that they were unaware of general moral obligations incumbent on individuals.

---

[12] See Martti Nissinen, ed., *Prophecy in its Ancient Near Eastern Context: Mesopotamian, Biblical, and Arabian Perspectives* (SBLSymS 13; Atlanta: Society of Biblical Literature, 2000).

Amos consistently assumes that people ought to recognize various moral norms, most of which have to do with what we call "social justice." Where he differs from his audience is in thinking that individuals' contravention of these norms spells disaster not just for the individuals in question but for the entire nation. For Amos, moral conduct rather than sacrifice is the touchstone of the relation between mortals and God, and it is clear from the book that this notion was found to be surprising. But the acknowledgement of certain moral norms, in itself, was widespread in Israelite society, as in any other, and Amos takes it for granted that the people are familiar with the moral principles he accuses them of breaching. He also assumes that they recognize these principles to be divinely given.

Most commentators have thought that the moral rules to which Amos appeals are derived from the "Book of the Covenant" in Exodus 21–23, which of all Israel's law codes has the best claim to have been the code in force in the eighth century, before the development of Deuteronomy or the Holiness Code (Leviticus 18–26). As we will see, nearly all the ethical norms Amos appeals to can be found in the Book of the Covenant, and it is reasonable to think that it was widely known in his day. As with the laws of any nation, people did not necessarily know it as a written code (most people were not literate), but its simple provisions may well have been widely taught by priests at sanctuaries, and it may have been the basis of moral instruction within the family. The force of Amos's condemnations would certainly have been diminished if people could say that they were simply unaware of the moral rules to which he appealed. But this is very unlikely. The Book of the Covenant, as is well known, agrees in many of its basic principles with ways of thinking about morality that were widespread throughout the ancient world, and which can also be found in the wisdom literature both of Israel and of other nations.[13] Probity in administering justice, fair weights and measures, respect for the poor, and avoidance of robbery and violent crime – all of these are the norms of most ancient as well as most modern societies, despite startling differences in detail, and they were clearly a given in Israel too. Amos's originality is not so much in pointing to the fact that people are breaching these norms, as in the fearful consequences he sees as following from that breach – namely, disaster for the whole nation. But Amos's contemporaries clearly knew the norms in question, and so he was reminding them of an existing moral code, not propounding a brand new one. The idea that these norms were the conditions in a kind of contract between the nation and God – which is what we generally mean by the term 'covenant' – was not widely shared, however, and so, at this point, Amos was probably introducing a new idea.

CONCLUSION

To conclude, it is possible to say quite a lot about the religious ideas and practices that form the background to the theological teaching of Amos and his circle, partly by extrapolation from Amos's own message and partly from what is known from other sources about religious thought and practice in the ancient Near East in general and in Israel in particular. It is against that background that we can now proceed to analyze the theology of the prophet and his followers, who gave us the core of the book as we now have it.

---

[13] See, e.g., Bernard S. Jackson, *Wisdom-Laws: A Study of the Mishpatim of Exodus 21:1–22:16* (Oxford: Oxford University Press, 2006); and David P. Wright, *Inventing God's Law: How the Covenant Code of the Bible Used and Revised the Laws of Hammurabi* (Oxford: Oxford University Press, 2009).

CHAPTER 3

The Theology of Amos and His Circle

Despite many of the arguments in Chapter 2, it would be a mistake to think that Amos's teaching was simply the negation of the religious assumptions of his audience, as though everything he said was totally original and unprecedented. As we have already seen, there were important areas in which he and his hearers clearly shared the same assumptions. Like them, for instance, Amos believed that the power of Yнwн extended over all nations of the world, and that he controlled the destinies of all. He also agreed that Yнwн would avenge atrocities committed in war, whoever committed them and against whomever they were committed. There was thus a wide base of theological agreement. Amos was not the first person in Israel to believe in the universal power of Yнwн, and thus there were already before his time signs of a kind of incipient monotheism.[1]

---

[1] For valuable discussions, see Mark S. Smith, *The Early History of God: Yahweh and the Other Deities in Ancient Israel* (2nd ed.; Grand Rapids: Eerdmans, 2002); idem, *God in Translation: Deities in Cross-Cultural Discourse in the Biblical World* (Grand Rapids: Eerdmans, 2010); Rainer Albertz, *A History of Israelite Religion in the Old Testament Period* (2 vols.; OTL; Louisville: Westminster John Knox, 1994); and John Day, *Yahweh and the Gods and Goddesses of Canaan* (JSOTSup 265; Sheffield: Sheffield Academic Press, 2002).

ISRAEL'S NON-ELECTION AND THE COMING DISASTER

The first thing we notice in the message of Amos is that he draws different conclusions from those drawn by his contemporaries from this agreed-upon universal power of the God of Israel. Two verses in particular stand out: Amos 3:2 and 9:7.

> You only have I known
> > of all the families of the earth;
> therefore I will punish you
> > for all your iniquities. (Amos 3:2)

> Are you not like the Ethiopians to me,
> > O people of Israel? says the LORD.
> Did I not bring Israel up from the land of Egypt,
> > and the Philistines from Caphtor and the Arameans from Kir?
> > (Amos 9:7)

The first of these verses appears to say that the exodus from Egypt and the giving of the Promised Land established that YHWH had a special relationship with Israel. He used his universal power in the interests of this one particular people, as it seems everyone in Israel in Amos's day believed already. But Amos draws from this the opposite conclusion from that drawn by his audience. For them, "YHWH is the God of Israel and Israel the people of YHWH" come what may, since in the exodus a relationship was forged that was permanent and unbreakable. For Amos, the special relationship with YHWH does not indemnify Israel, but rather makes them all the more culpable if they sin. The nature of God is not to be Israel's "helper," to use Wellhausen's formulation, but to be Israel's judge.[2]

---

[2]　Julius Wellhausen, *Prolegomena to the History of Ancient Israel with a Reprint of the Article Israel from the Encyclopaedia Britannica* (trans. J. S. Black and A. Menzies; repr. ed.; Cleveland: World Publishing, 1965), 469. See Chapter 2, note 2 herein.

The very fact that they have a special relationship with him gives them greater responsibility; it heightens their culpability if they disobey. The verse does not necessarily imply that the special bond with Yhwh is coming to an end, but it does overturn any sense of indemnification against punishment.

The second verse, 9:7, appears to say that a special relationship never existed in the first place. It is true that Yhwh brought Israel into Canaan from Egypt, but then he also brought the Philistines from Crete (Caphtor) and the Arameans from Kir. Precisely because Yhwh is a universal God, all the movements of the nations come about through his devising. There is nothing special about Israel in this regard, and, like any other nation, it will perish if it offends him:

> The eyes of the Lord are upon the sinful kingdom,
>> and I will destroy it from the face of the earth. (Amos 9:8a)

So, again, 9:7 appears to deny that there was ever anything unusual about Israel's relationship with Yhwh, which is an extremely startling message, scarcely if at all found anywhere else in the Old Testament. It is supported by 6:2–3:

> Cross over to Calneh, and see;
>> from there go to Hamath the great;
>> then go down to Gath of the Philistines.
> Are you better than these kingdoms?
>> or is your territory greater than their territory,
> O you that put far away the evil day,
>> and bring near a reign of violence?

Here, the prophet or his disciples appear to be saying that there is an equality between the Arameans, the Philistines, and Israel: none is better than another.[3]

---

[3]   The Hebrew text in fact says, "Are they better than these kingdoms? Or is their territory greater than your territory?' (see the notes in NRSV). The logic of

So far as 9:7 is concerned, it seems to me very difficult to think that it is not original to Amos himself. Using the principle of dissimilarity, we can argue that no one in later times would have attributed such a message to a prophet if there was not good reason to think he had expressed it himself. Israelite theology never developed the idea that there was nothing special about the relationship with Yhwh, but always asserted that Israel was God's chosen people. So if there is anything in Amos that must go back to the prophet himself, this is surely it. Does this mean then that 3:2, which softens the message – though only to the extent of saying that, just because Israel is special, it is all the more to blame! – is a later addition, even if already by the prophet's immediate disciples? It might be possible to reconcile the two sayings by suggesting that for Amos there was some real doubt about the election of Israel by Yhwh. If Israel was indeed Yhwh's special people, as everyone around him believed, then this had an implication that was the very opposite of what most people thought: it meant that Israel was even more blameworthy than other peoples. (This seems overall to be the message of the oracles against the nations.) On the other hand, it might be that there really never had been any special relationship in the first place, and in that case, Israel was at any rate just as much subject to punishment as any other people would have been. Israel is clearly damned either way, and perhaps the prophet was certain of that fact, but less sure about the theological

what is being said here seems to demand the NRSV's emendation of the text, and it is easy to see why a later scribe might have changed the original wording so as to imply that Israel is, after all, greater than these other states, but it is impossible to see why a scribe would have changed the text in the other direction so as to demote Israel. For that reason, I believe the NRSV has made the correct decision. See also Jörg Jeremias, *The Book of Amos: A Commentary* (trans. D. W. Stott; OTL; Louisville: Westminster John Knox, 1998 [German orig: 1995]), 108 n. 3.

underpinning of it. The practical conclusion is the same in both cases: heads I win, tails you lose.

But it may be, as Hadjiev argues, that Amos is unlikely to have been uncertain on a matter as central as the question of whether or not Israel and Yʜwʜ had a special relationship, and in that case, we should have to decide between the two sayings in 3:2 and 9:7 and attribute only one to the prophet himself.[4] The principle of dissimilarity would then argue strongly in favor of the authenticity of the less attractive saying. Amos 3:2, though remarkable enough on its own, does not actually deny the election of Israel, whereas – on the assumption that belief in the exodus implies belief in Israel's special status – it can be argued that 9:7 (backed by 6:2–3) does, and so it is the latter that should be regarded as authentic. It is less likely to have been invented because it is so contrary to later theological thinking. If that is so, then a central pillar of Amos's theology may be called the *non-election of Israel by Yʜwʜ*. Amos did not merely draw out unpalatable conclusions from Israel's special status, but actually denied that status altogether. The first theologian in Israel denied the very basis of all Israel's theology!

It is possible that Amos came to this conclusion over time, and that 3:2 represents an earlier, less radical Amos. A progression in Amos's thought was argued many years ago by Ernst Würthwein, who suggested that the vision cycle preserves evidence of development in Amos's thinking.[5] Amos began, according to him, as a cult prophet, a *Heilsnabi* ("prophet of salvation") in the normal ancient Near Eastern style, who gave oracles supportive of Israel

---

4 Tchavdar S. Hadjiev, *The Composition and Redaction of the Book of Amos* (BZAW 393; Berlin: Walter de Gruyter, 2009).
5 Ernst Würthwein, "Amos-Studien," *ZAW* 62 (1949–1950): 10–52.

and its kings. (As we have seen, more recent study of the prophets doubts whether official prophets always gave favorable oracles. Even though they did not predict judgment on the scale we find in Amos, they were not simply the king's yes-men.) Amos's first two visions represent the stage in his career at which he was already aware that all was not well with Israel and that it was threatened by Yhwh with punishment. But the visions convinced him that Yhwh was going to pardon it:

> This is what the Lord God showed me: he was forming locusts at the time the latter growth began to sprout (it was the latter growth after the king's mowings). When they had finished eating the grass of the land, I said,
>
> > "O Lord God, forgive, I beg you!
> > > How can Jacob stand?
> > > He is so small!"
> > The Lord relented concerning this;
> > > "It shall not be," said the Lord.
>
> This is what the Lord God showed me: the Lord God was calling for a shower of fire, and it devoured the great deep and was eating up the land. Then I said,
>
> > "O Lord God, cease, I beg you?
> > > How can Jacob stand?
> > > He is so small!"
> > The Lord relented concerning this;
> > > "This also shall not be," said the Lord. (Amos 7:1–6)

But the third vision, Würthwein suggested, comes from later in Amos's activity, and now he has reached the conviction that the time for forgiveness has passed, and the decree of destruction will not be revoked:

> This is what he showed me: the Lord was standing beside a wall built with a plumb line, with a plumb line in his hand. And the

LORD said to me, "Amos, what do you see?" And I said, "A plumb line." Then the Lord said,

> "See, I am setting a plumb line[6]
>> in the midst of my people Israel;
>> I will never again pass them by;
> The high places of Isaac shall be made desolate,
>> and the sanctuaries of Israel shall be laid waste,
>> and I will rise against the house of Jeroboam with the
>> sword." (Amos 7:7–9)

It was this revelation of judgment that, as the present arrangement of the book indicates, provoked the hostile reaction by Amaziah, the priest of Bethel, recorded in 7:10–17. Thereafter Amos uttered only oracles of judgment against Israel, as we see in the subsequent visions and the oracles attached to them: "Surely I will never forget any of their deeds" (8:7). Even if Würthwein's reconstruction is correct – and it is very speculative – then it would not wholly account for the move from 3:2 to 9:7, since both speak of judgment, not salvation. But it would allow us to think of Amos as having developed his ideas over time, and thus make space for two oracles that are admittedly not wholly compatible with each other as both genuinely going back to the prophet himself.

Whatever we make of all this, the question of Israel's "election" by YHWH is clearly a central issue for Amos, and it is perhaps here that he is most radical and most unacceptable to later tradition. Indeed, as we will see, his message was duly toned down in the generations that followed. His overwhelming conviction is that the nation faces a destructive judgment by YHWH, from which no amount of appeals to its special status can save it.

---

[6] The meaning of the Hebrew here is much discussed: if "plumb line" is correct, then the image is of YHWH testing the wall that represents Israel, and, finding that it is out of plumb, deciding on its demolition.

NATIONAL SIN

Why is the nation doomed? Here again, Amos is clearly original in
his teaching. The judgment that is impending has nothing to do, as
people in the ancient Near East generally believed, with neglect of
the gods through failure to sacrifice properly. On the contrary, as
we will see, Amos believes there has been too much sacrifice, not
too little. The sins that have caused YHWH to decide on judgment
are concerned almost exclusively with how people behave toward
each other. Here are some salient examples.

1. *Amos 2:6–8* specifies a number of offenses against what we
should perhaps call social justice:[7]

> Thus says the LORD:
> For three transgressions of Israel,
>   and for four, I will not revoke the punishment;
> because they sell the righteous for silver,
>   and the needy for a pair of sandals –
> they who trample the head of the poor into the dust of the earth,
>   and push the afflicted out of the way;
> father and son go into the same girl,
>   so that my holy name is profaned;
> they lay themselves down by every altar
>   on garments taken in pledge,
> and in the house of their God they drink
>   wine bought with fines they imposed.

Not all of the offenses specified here are absolutely clear, though
the general thrust is plain enough. "Selling the righteous" may
mean selling innocent people into debt slavery, with the "pair
of sandals" indicating that this is done when the debt owed is as

---

[7] See the very useful work by Léon Epsztein, *Social Justice in the Ancient Near
East and the People of the Bible* (trans. J. Bowden; London: SCM, 1986 [French
orig: 1983]).

trivial as the price of sandals; or it may mean "selling" in a more metaphorical sense, taking bribes to convict people, in which case the point would be that the judges are so corrupt that even the price of a pair of sandals is enough to buy their verdict. In either case, the object of the prophet's attack is the ruling classes, the rich and powerful. The same is true in the next verse, where they "trample the head of the poor into the dust of the earth," even though the Hebrew may be somewhat corrupt here. Then we have what is probably mainly an attack on the exploitation of female slaves (the "girl" probably being a servant), to such an extent that men are not afraid to commit what amounts to incest with the women they abuse.[8] "Garments taken in pledge," that is, in pawn, were supposed to be returned to their owner before sundown according to Exodus 22:26–27 – the theory probably being that if one pledged one's outer garment it was the last thing one had, the only thing that could be used as bedclothes. The reference to fines again implies that judges are in view, and that they fine people simply to fund their own drinking. (The lines "by every altar" and "in the house of their God" are thought by some to be later additions, turning social injustice into blasphemy.)[9] The picture we get is of a fairly typical ancient (or indeed modern) society, with bribery and corruption endemic, and the rich and influential oppressing

---

[8]   For the possibility that "the girl" is really a place name (Naarah), see the article by Sharon Moughtin-Mumby, "'A Man and His Father Go to Naarah in order to Defile My Holy Name': Rereading Amos 2.6–8," in *Aspects of Amos: Exegesis and Interpretation* (eds. A. C. Hagedorn and A. Mein; LHBOTS 536; London: T & T Clark, 2011), 59–82.

[9]   On all the details in this oracle, see Hans Walter Wolff, *Joel and Amos: A Commentary on the Books of the Prophets Joel and Amos* (trans. W. Janzen, S. D. McBride, Jr., and C. A. Muenchow; ed. S. D. McBride, Jr.; Hermeneia; Philadelphia: Fortress, 1977 [German orig.: 1969]), 167–168; and Jeremias, *Amos*, 37–38.

and exploiting the weak and poor. There is no particular reason to think that Israelite society had only recently developed these features in the eighth century BCE, though it may have done so. Rather, what is new is the presence of a prophet to denounce them, and to proclaim that they are bad enough sins to explain the coming downfall of the whole country when the Assyrians invade.

2. *Amos 3:10* condemns injustice again:

> They do not know how to do right,
>   says the LORD,
> those who store up violence
>   and robbery in their strongholds.

There is nothing very specific here, but the same general picture emerges, and for the first time, a generalizing term for virtuous action – "right" (Hebrew *nĕkōḥâ*) – which is being violated.

3. In *Amos 4:1*, there is an attack on the women of Samaria:

> Hear this word, you cows of Bashan
>   who are on Mount Samaria,
> who oppress the poor, who crush the needy,
>   who say to their husbands, "Bring something to drink!"

Addressing the women as "cows" may not have been derogatory in itself: terms of endearment are notoriously hard to evaluate, and the comparison with the particularly well-fed cows in Transjordan may have been a compliment. Whether it was or not, the oracle as a whole is clearly sharply critical of the wives of Israel's rich men, interested – like the judges in 2:8 – only in extracting money from the already poor in order to be able to drink. Drunkenness, especially at the expense of the needy, is a stock theme in later prophecy too (cf. Isa 5:22; 28:1–13).

4. *Amos 5:10–12* continues the same themes as the Israel oracle in chapter 2:

> They hate the one who reproves in the gate,
>> and they abhor the one who speaks the truth.
> Therefore, because you trample on the poor,
>> and take from them levies of grain,
> you have built houses of hewn stone,
>> but you shall not live in them;
> you have planted pleasant vineyards,
>> but you shall not drink their wine.
> For I know how many are your transgressions,
>> and how great are your sins –
> you who afflict the righteous, who take a bribe,
>> and push aside the needy in the gate.

The space inside the gate was the place where courts sat and the town council met in Israelite towns and cities, and it is with what goes on there that Amos is concerned in this oracle. Bribery and corruption are again the theme. All the cultures of the ancient Near East had teaching about the need for social justice, often contained in the respective culture's wisdom literature, and all of them clearly needed such instruction. Israel in the eighth century was probably no better or worse than other countries, but that, in the prophet's eyes, was bad enough, and he threatens them with what is sometimes called a "futility curse" in which everything they attempt comes to nothing.

5. The excessive luxury of the rich, as Amos saw it, is condemned in *Amos 6:4–6*:

> Alas for those who lie in beds of ivory,
>> and lounge on their couches,
> and eat lambs from the flock,
>> and calves from the stall;
> who sing idle songs to the sound of the harp,
>> and like David improvise on instruments of music,
> who drink wine from bowls,
>> and anoint themselves with the finest oils,
>> but are not grieved over the ruin of Joseph!

There is a clearly ascetic element in the make-up of all the great prophets, turning away with disgust from what they see as too much luxury. Again, it is important to see here that Amos is not concerned with luxury in and of itself, but with what it contrasts with: in the earlier oracles with the exploitation of the poor, and here with indifference to the coming fate of the nation ("the ruin of Joseph"). Older commentators sometimes presented him as a simple country dweller from the poorer kingdom of Judah outraged by the affluence he saw in Samaria, but that is essentially unknowable. The picture he himself presents is of a reasoned opposition to luxury in the face of widespread poverty and national complacency, not a cultural reaction to unaccustomed riches.

6. In *Amos 6:12*, we have the first case where the prophecy explicates what is wrong about wrongdoing:

> Do horses run on rocks?
>> Does one plough the sea with oxen?
> But you have turned justice into poison,
>> and the fruit of righteousness into wormwood.

We meet here a pair of terms, "justice" and "righteousness," which in the prophets often serve as shorthand for what we have been calling social justice. Note also 5:24 (italics added):

> Let *justice* roll down like waters,
>> and *righteousness* like an ever-flowing stream.

The existence of such terms shows that the prophets, and Amos first among them, could sum up in a generalizing formula the various rules about how people ought to behave toward each other that he saw being infringed. But the first half of the verse shows that he had also thought about why certain actions were wrong: they were as absurd as trying to ride over rocks or plough the sea. What we have here is a sense that the national sin is *unnatural*. The natural world obeys certain orders – animals have preset boundaries, and certain activities are impossible – but Israel knows no natural bounds in its conduct. There is a very similar oracle in Isaiah 1:3:

> The ox knows its owner
> > and the donkey its master's crib;
> but Israel does not know,
> > my people do not understand.

Jeremiah also refers to the orders observed by birds and natural phenomena, contrasting them unfavorably with the behavior of Israel:

> Even the stork in the heavens
> > knows its times;
> and the turtle-dove, swallow, and crane
> > observe the time of their coming;
> but my people do not know
> > the ordinance of the LORD. (Jer 8:7)
>
> Does the snow of Lebanon
> > leave the crags of Sirion?
> Do the mountain waters run dry,
> > the cold flowing streams?
> But my people have forgotten me. (Jer 18:14–15)

All this tends to cast the social justice required of Israel in the guise of a kind of "natural morality" rather than as a set of divine ordinances. This does not mean that it does not ultimately derive from God, since God is the giver of all the orders of the world in any case, but it does mean that Amos may not be appealing to *divine law* to back up his claims, but more to moral inclinations he thinks are (or ought to be) common to people just as human beings.

7. The final oracle about social justice is in *Amos 8:4–6*, which may be an authentic word of Amos or his circle, or may be a later summary of his teaching:

> Hear this, you that trample on the needy,
>   and bring to ruin the poor of the land,
> saying, "When will the new moon be over,
>   so that we may sell grain,
> and the sabbath,
>   so that we may offer wheat for sale.
> We will make the ephah small and the shekel great,
>   and practice deceit with false balances,
> buying the poor for silver,
>   and the needy for a pair of sandals,
>   and selling the sweepings of the wheat."

Apart from the repetition of 2:6 in the last verse, there is new material here: a condemnation of sharp practice in the market, with false weights and measures designed to cheat people. The shopkeepers denounced here – in this case not the ruling classes, therefore – are portrayed as longing for the sabbath and new moon to be over so that they can open their shops again, evidence that these were days when commerce stopped. Again, Amos presents those he denounces as primarily to blame for oppressing the poor and needy.

In many cases, the moral norms that are being transgressed can be found in the Book of the Covenant (Exod 21–23), but are also often found in the wisdom literature. Here are some examples:

> You shall not pervert the justice due to your poor in their lawsuits. Keep far from a false charge, and do not kill the innocent or those in the right, for I will not acquit the guilty. You shall take no bribe, for a bribe blinds the officials, and subverts the cause of those who are in the right. (Exod 23:6–8)

> Do not rob the poor because they are poor,
>   or crush the afflicted at the gate;

for the LORD pleads their cause,
    and despoils of life those who despoil them. (Prov 22:22–23)

It would be misleading, however, or at least unjustified, to say that Amos is condemning his contemporaries for breaking the law or, for that matter, for infringing principles taught in wisdom circles. He nowhere appeals to any overarching concept such as lawbreaking or even "folly" (as Isaiah will later do), though we have seen that he does use the summarizing phrase "justice and righteousness." Amos simply states the crime in each case, and we have no way of knowing whether he had any kind of theory about why particular infractions are wrong. They are, to use the term favored in the oracles against the nations, *pěšāʿîm* (פשעים) a general word for sin or misdemeanor that contains no particular ethical theory within itself.[10] The emphasis seems to fall more on a kind of self-evidence about the moral norms being transgressed: people simply ought to know (from whatever source) that these things are wrong. An instructive contrast can be seen in the (secondary) oracle against Judah in 2:4–5, where it is said that the Judeans have "rejected the law of the LORD, and have not kept his statutes." There is nothing like this in the rest of Amos.

CONDEMNATION OF THE SACRIFICIAL CULT

There are other surprises in Amos's moral condemnations, in particular his attitude to the cult with its offering of sacrifices. Amos 4:4–5 derides the sacrificial cult at Bethel and Gilgal by sarcastically telling the people to heap up their sacrifices:

---

[10] See the discussion in Rolf P. Knierim, *Die Hauptbegriffe für Sünde im Alten Testament* (Gütersloh: Gütersloher Verlagshaus, 1965).

Come to Bethel – and transgress,
    to Gilgal – and multiply transgression;
bring your sacrifices every morning,
    your tithes every three days;
bring a thank-offering of leavened bread,
    and proclaim free-will offerings, publish them;
for so you love to do, O people of Israel!
                    says the Lord GOD.

Later in the book, God is presented as denouncing the festivals
(5:21–24):

I hate, I despise your festivals,
    and I take no delight in your solemn assemblies.
Even though you offer me your burnt-offerings and grain-offerings
    I will not accept them,
and the offerings of well being of your fatted animals
    I will not look upon.
Take away from me the noise of your songs;
    I will not listen to the melody of your harps.
But let justice roll down like water,
    and righteousness like an ever-flowing stream.

Even if 5:25, as we have seen, is probably later than Amos himself, it captures Amos's sense that sacrifice was not part of YHWH's original desires for how Israel ought to behave:

Did you bring to me sacrifices and offerings the forty years in the wilderness, O house of Israel?

Opposition to sacrifice is very striking in the ancient context. In later times, the Greek philosophical tradition came to regard sacrifice as unnecessary, but no ancient religion known to us was non-sacrificial in character. This is so remarkable that some scholars have argued that it is a misunderstanding of Amos to suppose that he can have had a root-and-branch opposition to sacrifice. Perhaps he meant that the sacrifices were being offered to the wrong god, or that the Israelites had their priorities wrong: they were correct to think that Yнwн required sacrifice, mistaken to think that it took precedence over the "weightier matters" of the law such as justice between persons. This problem needs further examination.[11]

It may be argued that the preexilic prophets were in reality far less badly disposed toward cultic religion than the texts, taken at face value, might seem to suggest (together with the relevant verses in Amos, compare also Isa 1:10–17; Jer 6:20; 7:22; Hos 6:6; Micah 6:6–7). One line of argument is that it is simply not conceivable that anyone in ancient Israel could have been so radically anti-ritualistic as these texts seem to imply. Religion, it is suggested, was so intimately bound up with sacrifice and ritual that no one could have opposed them per se without stepping outside the culture altogether. Sometimes this point is linked to the speculation that finding anti-ritualistic attitudes in the prophets reflects a characteristically Protestant agenda, that issues to do with disputes between Protestants and Catholics are being read back into the Old Testament, and that this is anachronistic. There can be little doubt, for instance, that Wellhausen's opposition to ritual in religion, which he regarded as a somewhat degenerate phenomenon, is linked to his liberal Protestantism.[12]

---

[11] For what follows, see John Barton, "The Prophets and the Cult," in *Temple and Worship in Biblical Israel* (ed. J. Day; LHBOTS 422; London: T & T Clark, 2005), 111–122.

[12] See the discussion in John Barton, "Wellhausen's *Prolegomena to the History of Israel*: Influences and Effects," in *Text and Experience: Towards a Cultural Exegesis of the Bible* (ed. Daniel Smith-Christopher; BS 35; Sheffield: Sheffield Academic Press, 1995), 316–319, reprinted in idem, *The Old Testament: Canon, Literature and Theology: Collected Essays of John Barton* (Aldershot: Ashgate, 2007), 169–179. See also the essays gathered in *Semeia* 25 (1982): *Julius Wellhausen and His Prolegomena to the History of Israel* (ed. Douglas A. Knight); as well as Bryan D. Bibb, "The Prophetic Critique of Ritual in Old Testament Theology," in *The Priests in the Prophets: The Portrayal of Priests,*

Similarly, Jewish readers sometimes see the emphasis on the anti-ritualism of the prophets as part of a general Christian opposition to the ritual side of Judaism, proceeding from a contrast between a dead religion of external works and a living religion of the heart, which they feel is a denigration of Judaism that looks for support from the prophets but in the process remakes the prophets in its own image. Probably the easiest way to reconcile such a defense of ritual in religion against which the prophets appear to be arguing is to say that they were not speaking against cultic ritual in principle, but rather wanted to introduce an order of priorities. Sacrifice is not unacceptable in itself, but is simply of a lower order of importance than social justice or heartfelt repentance. Thus we read Hosea's "I desire steadfast love and not sacrifice" (Hos 6:6) as "I desire steadfast love *in the first place* and sacrifice *only in the second place*," or "I desire steadfast love *more than* I desire sacrifice, though it goes without saying that I do also desire sacrifice." Similarly, Joel's "Rend your hearts and not your clothing" (Joel 2:13) means "Rend your hearts *as well as* your clothing," or "Let your torn clothing represent *true inward contrition* – but tear it all the same." This is far from impossible, and would be reminiscent of what Jesus is reported as saying in Matthew's Gospel:

> Woe to you, scribes and Pharisees, hypocrites! For you tithe mint, dill, and cumin, and have neglected the weightier matters of the law: justice and mercy and faith. It is these you ought to have practiced *without neglecting the others*. (Matt 23:23)

Both-and, rather than *either-or*, would be the essence of the prophetic message in this interpretation.

Prophets and Other Religious Specialists in the Latter Prophets (eds. Lester L. Grabbe and Alice Ogden Bellis; LHBOTS 408; London: T & T Clark, 2004), 31–43.

Another possible line of argument is that the prophets were opposed to ritual not in itself, but rather when offered by those with hands polluted by crime. This can claim some support from Isaiah 1:15, "When you stretch out your hands I will hide my eyes from you; even though you make many prayers I will not listen; *your hands are full of blood.*" This does not imply a root-and-branch opposition to the cult, but only the (surely widely shared) belief that those who offer sacrifice must be in a state of purity, and moral transgression – especially such sins as murder or theft – pollute would-be worshippers just as much as offenses against purity regulations do, and make their sacrifices unacceptable. Compare Malachi 3:3–4, where the offerings made by the Levites need purification, but there is no question of opposition to religious ritual as such.

As a third possibility, it may be argued that the prophets were often cultic officials themselves, so that it is inconceivable that they could have opposed the sacrificial cultus as such, and hence some other explanation must be found for their condemnations of sacrifice. This has been a characteristic argument in Scandinavian scholarship, where a cultic setting for much in the Old Testament has been typically more popular than in German or Anglo-Saxon realms. One might think, for instance, of Hans M. Barstad's work on Amos, *The Religious Polemics of Amos*, which sees Amos as a cult prophet, rather than as the outsider to Israelite institutions postulated by traditional German-speaking scholarship.[13] It is of a piece with this that when faced with Amos 5:25, "Did you bring me sacrifices and offerings forty years in the wilderness?," Barstad argues that the emphasis must fall on "me": Was it *to me* that you offered your sacrifices during the forty years in the wilderness? The

---

[13]   Hans M. Barstad, *The Religious Polemics of Amos: Studies in the Preaching of Am. 2,7B–8; 4,1–13; 5,1–27; 6,4–7; 8,14* (VTSup 34; Leiden: Brill 1984).

assumed answer is: "No, it was to other gods." Thus the prophetic polemic against sacrifice is really a polemic against *false* worship. This is often so in Hosea, as most scholars would probably agree, but Barstad sees it as normal throughout the prophetic corpus. Prophetic opposition to sacrifice is thus opposition to syncretism, not to cultic activity as such.

The problem with this position is that it does not seem to do justice to the assertion in Jeremiah 7:27 that YHWH had never commanded sacrifice at all, nor to Amos's own insistence that he hated Israel's feasts not because they were celebrated in honor of the wrong god but because they were unaccompanied by justice and righteousness. As many scholars have argued, it is hard to defend the picture of Amos as actually a cultic prophet when so much that he says tends to undermine not just a syncretized cult but any cult at all. Even if he was originally a cultic prophet, as Würthwein and others supposed[14] – an interpretation that is now not widely supported – Amos seems to have changed his mind by the time he produced the oracles we have been looking at. Even a mild degree of criticism of the cult would sit badly with a true cultic prophet, and the level of invective against the cult in the book of Amos can hardly be compatible with the prophet holding an official position within the cult.

For the theoretical question of whether it is conceivable that anyone in an ancient society could have been as anti-cultic as Amos appears to be, we may look at the work of Mary Douglas, especially her book *Natural Symbols*.[15] There Douglas deals at length with the

[14] Würthwein, "Amos-Studien"; see also Henning Graf Reventlow, *Das Amt des Propheten bei Amos* (FRLANT 80; Göttingen: Vandenhoeck & Ruprecht, 1962).

[15] Mary Douglas, *Natural Symbols: Explorations in Cosmology* (London: Penguin, 1970).

phenomenon of anti-ritualism in religion and shows that it is by no means a product only of a modern, secularized culture, but occurs equally in what she (still) refers to as "primitive" societies. It is not in the least unusual to find groups living within, or alongside, a highly ritualized society that reject virtually all ritual activities or reduce their ritual to a bare minimum, stressing inner experience and freedom of religious expression. This is true, according to her, of the religious culture of pygmies as against the cultures of the groups with which the pygmies coexist. Those who thus reject ritual are characteristically those who are alienated from the values of a larger group, but this may be because they are outcasts or of low social status, or because they are highly distinctive individuals, who, as it were, plow their own furrow, and perhaps attract a following that picks up and imitates their own anti-ritualistic cast of mind. In Douglas's words:

> Alienation from the current social values usually takes a set form: a denunciation not only of irrelevant rituals, but of ritualism as such; exaltation of the inner experience and denigration of its standardized expressions; preference for intuitive and instant forms of knowledge; rejection of mediating institutions, rejection of any tendency to allow habit to provide the basis of a new symbolic system.[16]

That the classical prophets of Israel could be seen in this light seems clear enough, and so it is not necessarily an anachronism to paint them in the colors of Protestant reformers. There is a clear similarity in some of the attitudes expressed.

Douglas also points out that anti-ritualism may go hand-in-hand with a stress on the superior importance of "good works" in the sense of a commitment to charity and to social justice. Her particular example is taken from London of the 1960s when, in the

---

[16] Ibid., 40.

wake of the Second Vatican Council, Catholic clergy were often themselves somewhat anti-ritualistic, and spent much energy in trying to persuade their people that such ritualized observances as Friday abstinence from meat should be replaced with acts of generosity to those in need – the kind of "true fast," in fact, proposed by Trito-Isaiah in Isaiah 58. This plea was unheeded, in fact virtually unheard, by Irish manual workers who, in their exile in alien London, held fast to Friday abstinence as a defining mark of their Catholic culture, and resisted the attempts by the Catholic intelligentsia to deritualize their religious practice. No doubt the lines of this discord have changed greatly in the intervening forty years or so, but Douglas's point, which is that ritualistic and anti-ritualistic opinions can occur within the same general religious culture, remains an important one. Her own sympathies are very much with the Irish laborers; she has little time for a "prophetic" religion that would remove people's ritual markers. But she is quite clear that prophetic types of religion do indeed occur within traditional cultures, and – though she does not directly refer to the Old Testament prophets – her arguments support the theoretical possibility that they too could have been as anti-cultic as they appear to be. Nothing in cultural anthropology precludes the possibility at any rate.

Amos even uses a cultic term, "seek" in an anti-cultic way, in 5:4–5, where "seeking" YHWH is actually contrasted with "seeking" Bethel and Gilgal, which means to offer sacrifices there. True "seeking" of God is not expressed in cultic actions, but in practicing justice and righteousness (5:7). Thus Amos sets his face against cultic religion. Whether he thought there could be circumstances under which it would be acceptable, and whether he would have distinguished, for example, between the offering of sacrifices and a non-sacrificial liturgy, there is no way of telling. The latter option, in particular, was apparently not available. Clearly, Amos was not against what might be called "verbal" (non-sacrificial) prayer, since he practices it himself in 7:2 and 7:5. But all the prophets presuppose that it is possible to communicate with God through words. What the preexilic prophets at least seem to oppose is the offering of physical objects – animal carcasses and cereals – at Yhwh's shrines, as though these were *substitutes* for behaving rightly toward other people. No doubt these prophets would have had opponents who would have argued that this was to misunderstand the nature of sacrificial worship, just as anyone who uses symbols in worship is likely to regard Deutero-Isaiah's idol polemics as essentially unfair. But such voices are not heard in the book of Amos.

REPENTANCE AND SALVATION?

So far, I have presented Amos's message as essentially one of doom – unremitting disaster that will befall the whole nation. And there is plenty in the book to support such a reading:

> An adversary shall surround the land,
>   and strip you of your defense;
>   and your strongholds shall be plundered. (Amos 3:11)

> On the day I punish Israel for its transgressions,
>   I will punish the altars of Bethel,
> and the horns of the altar shall be cut off
>   and fall to the ground.
> I will tear down the winter house as well as the summer house;
>   and the houses of ivory shall perish,
> and the great houses shall come to an end,
>   says the LORD. (Amos 3:14–15)

> Fallen, no more to rise,
>   is maiden Israel;
> forsaken on her land,
>   with no one to raise her up.

For thus says the Lord God:
The city that marched out a thousand
        shall have a hundred left,
and that which marched out a hundred
        shall have ten left. (Amos 5:2–3)

If ten people remain in one house, they shall die. And if a relative, one who burns the dead, shall take up the body to bring it out of the house, and shall say to someone in the innermost parts of the house, "Is anyone else with you?" the answer will come, "No." Then the relative shall say, "Hush! We must not mention the name of the Lord." (Amos 6:9–10)

There are, however, two interrelated questions that might lead us to soften the picture somewhat. First, did Amos preach repentance? And, second, did he think that, if repentance was forthcoming, it was possible that the disaster could be averted? These are questions that arise for all the preexilic prophets, but they are specially acute in the case of Amos because his oracles are so particularly bleak. Whereas Hosea seems at least to envision a hope beyond judgment, and Isaiah has passages that speak of possible ways of avoiding doom, Amos is very largely pessimistic in tone. Even so, it is possible that the picture is not quite as dark as it seems.

In different places, each of which quite possibly reflects authentic words of the prophet, Amos calls on Israel to "seek" Yhwh (5:4; 5:6; 5:14), and (as we saw above) he makes it clear that this "seeking" is not to be done through the sacrificial cult, but through a reformation of behavior toward others. Would the prophet have said this if he had thought that there was no possibility that his hearers would respond or that, if they did, Yhwh would simply ignore them? A major emphasis in some German Old Testament scholarship, perhaps best summed up in Rudolf Smend's essay "Das Nein des Amos" ("Amos's No") has been that the calls to repentance are not to be taken very seriously.[17] They are statements of what could have saved the day, but that possibility is now already in the past and thus over.

In favor of Smend's interpretation is the clear fact that Amos hardly ever (if at all) tells people what to do. What form critics call the *Mahnwort* (word of exhortation) is conspicuously absent everywhere except in these three passages. Amos tells the people what they have done wrong in the past and are doing wrong in the present, but does not present them with any options for reform in the future. The moral condemnations that we have discussed above are not instructions to behave better, but retrospective analyses of what is wrong in the national life and why, therefore, disaster is impending. This means that the prophet's aim is not moral exhortation but theodicy, the attempt to explain (imminent) suffering and to get people to accept it as divine punishment.

Against such an interpretation, it may be said that, first, on the face of it, these three texts are genuine calls to repentance, and, second, it is difficult to understand why the prophet should have prophesied at all if there was now no chance of averting the disaster. The logic of prophecy is that there is a glimmer of light.[18] The rhetoric of prophecy is to say "All is lost, it's too late" precisely to get people to take the call to amendment with utmost seriousness. Prophecies of the final hour are always really prophecies of

---

[17] Rudolf Smend, "Das Nein des Amos," *EvT* 23 (1963): 404–423; repr. in idem, *Die Mitte des Alten Testaments* (BEvT 99; Munich: Kaiser, 1986), 85–103.

[18] See the persuasive arguments of Karl Möller, *A Prophet in Debate: The Rhetoric of Persuasion in the Book of Amos* (JSOTSup 372; Sheffield: Sheffield Academic Press, 2003). Note also Abraham J. Heschel, *The Prophets* (New York: Perennial Classics, 2001 [orig. 1962]), esp. 365–368, on the contingency of divine wrath and its instrumental, not stative, nature – that is, "[i]ts meaning is ... to bring about repentance; its purpose and consummation is its own disappearance."

the eleventh hour, predicting unavoidable disaster just so that it becomes avoidable, because the audience, finally stung into action, will manage to make a last-minute move in the direction that will save them. Most English-speaking scholarship, and some German scholarship too, has taken this line. Indeed, it has been argued that defending the hardline belief that for Amos there was literally no hope is part of a Protestant interpretation of the prophets that wants them to have taught the total depravity of the human person, and that Catholic or Jewish interpreters would never have produced such a totally unhopeful reading of the text.[19] If that is correct, then even Amos, prophet of doom that he was, did harbor at least a slight hope that all was really not yet lost, and his three exhortations to "seek" YHWH bear witness to this glimmer of light. This is not to say that the full-blown hope for a restoration *after* disaster that we find in the epilogue is at all likely to be authentic; that is another matter altogether. It is simply to doubt whether an entirely hopeless message could ever plausibly have been delivered (or received). It is clear, as we have seen, that prophets in the ancient Near East usually did not deliver such devoid-of-hope messages, and even among the preexilic prophets, Amos is almost alone in scarcely even hinting at better possibilities to come. So perhaps he is ever so slightly more hopeful than he seems?

To resolve this question, we have to consider another first. Which came first for the prophets: the analysis of social wrongdoing or the conviction of coming judgment? English-speaking scholarship, and also most Jewish scholarship, has tended to emphasize the first. The prophets are seen as social critics – in this,

---

[19] This is argued in Othmar Keel, "Rechttun oder Annahme des drohenden Gerichts?" *BZ* 21 (1977): 200–218. Compare the remarks above about possible Protestant bias in the understanding of prophetic attacks on the cult.

they were so unlike the majority of ancient Near Eastern prophets
that the title "prophet" may not be very suitable for them: E. W.
Heaton famously described them as "morally sensitive laymen."[20]
On the basis of their trenchant analysis of the moral state of the
nation, they became convinced that YHWH was bound to punish
it, and looking for possible means by which this might occur, their
sensitive antennae picked up the hints of growing Assyrian power.
Indeed, by the time of Isaiah, the Assyrian threat was obvious, but
in the case of Amos, who lived in a time of prosperity, it required
real insight to see that it was indeed the Assyrians that YHWH would
use as instruments of punishment. (Conceivably, Amos may have
thought that a resurgence of Aramean power would be the chosen
means of destruction.) The idea that the essence of a prophet is
to be a social critic rather than a kind of clairvoyant who foresees
the future is deeply entrenched in English-language writing about
the prophets, and it is classically expressed in the contrast between
"foretelling" (which, it was thought, the prophets did not have as
their primary task) and "forthtelling," that is, announcing to the
people their social injustices and offenses. Compare Micah 3:8:

> But as for me, I am filled with power,
>   with the spirit of the LORD,
>   and with justice and might,
> to declare to Jacob his transgressions,
>   and to Israel his sin.

But ever since the work of Wellhausen, a strong strand in German
scholarship has argued instead that what came first in the prophetic
consciousness was the awareness of impending doom.[21] The

---

[20] E. W. Heaton, *The Old Testament Prophets* (Atlanta: John Knox, 1977), 36.

[21] Both Hans Walter Wolff and Klaus Koch are salient examples – see the discussion in A. Vanlier Hunter, *Seek the Lord! A Study of the Meaning and Purpose
of the Exhortations in Amos, Hosea, Isaiah, Micah, and Zephaniah* (Baltimore:

prophets of ancient Israel were like the prophets of other ancient cultures in being focused primarily on the future – granted, not the remote "messianic" future of the popular Christian under-standing of Old Testament prophecy, but the future nevertheless, particularly the immediate and terrible future from which there was no escape. The prophets themselves saw their message about impending disaster as given by Yʜwʜ through revelation, but there is nothing to prevent us from tracing it to their own sensi-tivity for the signs of the times, just as their social analysis can be traced to their moral sensitivity. The important point is that it was the awareness of what the future held that prompted the prophets to speak out. Their moral analysis can then be seen as a kind of rational explanation of *why* the future is so bleak. Unlike ordinary prophets in the ancient world, the prophets of Israel were not mere mouthpieces for divine predictions, but thought in terms of rea-sons for the bleakness of their message. They wanted to tell people not simply *that* all was lost, but *why* it was. They argued that the coming disaster was not the result of a capricious decision on the part of an irrational god, but instead was fully justified in the light of all that Yʜwʜ's people had done to offend him. In other words, their task was to produce a theodicy, a moral justification for God's acting as they were convinced he would, and to try to persuade their hearers to accept it.[22]

But why bother with that in the first place? In the Old Testament more generally, the quest for meaning amidst the sufferings of Israel's history is often evident. It can be argued that the entire

St Mary's Seminary & University, 1982). Another example may be found in Werner H. Schmidt, *Zukunftsgewissheit und Gegenwartskritik: Grundzüge prophetischer Verkündigung* (2nd ed.; Neukirchen-Vluyn: Neukirchener Verlag, 2002 [orig: 1973]).

[22] For a powerful argument along these lines, see Vanlier Hunter, *Seek the Lord*.

"Deuteronomistic History," the story of Israel in the books of Joshua, Judges, 1–2 Samuel, and 1–2 Kings, has as its purpose the explanation of why the history took the course it did. These books are not written to glorify Israel, as many other ancient works of historiography were written to glorify the nations that produced them, but to "justify the ways of God to man" (Milton's classic formulation of the nature of theodicy). These books exist to bear witness to the human sin that led YHWH to visit terrible punishments on his own people. Perhaps that is also the purpose of early prophetic collections, such as the first edition of Amos, and perhaps it was also the purpose of the prophet Amos himself.

But there is a paradox here. If we want to ask, "Why bother prophesying if all is lost anyway?" we could equally well ask, "Why construct a theodicy, which presents God as just and justified in his punishment, when there is going to be no future in which to benefit from this realization?" The answer may be because, like a poetic lament, such a theodicy constitutes a way of acknowledging that God is good as well as powerful. And from there, it is only a small step to asking such a good God to step in and improve the plight of his admittedly sinful people. In penitential texts, for example, guilt is recognized as a way of asking God to be merciful:[23]

> For I know my transgressions,
>> and my sin is ever before me.
> Against you, you alone, have I sinned,
>> and done what is evil in your sight,
> so that you are justified in your sentence,
>> and blameless when you pass judgment ...

---

[23] See, among others, Mark J. Boda, "The Priceless Gain of Penitence: From Communal Lament to Penitential Prayer in the 'Exilic' Liturgy of Israel," in *Lamentations in Ancient and Contemporary Cultural Contexts* (eds. Nancy C. Lee and Carleen Mandolfo; SBLSymS 43; Atlanta: Society of Biblical Literature, 2008), 81–101 (with extensive literature).

Create in me a clean heart, O God,
> and put a new and right spirit within me.
Do not cast me away from your presence,
> and do not take your holy spirit from me.
Restore to me the joy of your salvation,
> and sustain in me a willing spirit. (Ps 51:3–4, 10–12)

So in the end, there *is* some hope, after all. But it lies not in an immediate expectation that God will avert disaster, but in a sense of trust that *on the other side of disaster* there may still be a future. Such an approach does not think that the disaster can be avoided, but does trust that God may still have gracious purposes beyond it (or through it). This is essentially the argument of the book of Hosea in its finished form, and it is also, as we will see, the message that the book of Amos communicates. But it could be that even Amos himself was not blind to this way of thinking. If that is the case, we can in a sense have our cake and eat it too: the totally unhopeful message still contains within itself the seeds of hope! This is not because the prophet thought people would heed his warnings and repent; it was because the prophet believed that YHWH was ultimately merciful, though his people would still have to pass through dire suffering, a suffering that could not now be averted, on the way – perhaps – to eventual restoration in some as yet unimaginable form.

While seeing the force of the argument that prophets do not prophesy if they have no hope at all, I thus believe that the line of interpretation that reaches back from Smend to Wellhausen has the weight of evidence on its side. This can be supported if we turn from using general, theoretical terms such as "repentance," "disaster," and "restoration," and focus on the realities of Amos's day. Amos was convinced, by whatever means, that Israel faced extinction: not necessarily in the sense that no single Israelite would survive (a very unlikely outcome in ancient warfare), but in the sense that there would no longer be an Israel as a sovereign and prosperous nation. He may have thought that this would come about at the hands of the Arameans, but it is more likely that, like his younger contemporary Isaiah, he saw the Assyrians as the great threat. In the 760s or 750s, this was a prescient though not necessarily a supernatural insight. He concluded – and in this, he was highly original – that the expected Assyrian invasion, which would sweep away the other nations of the region as well as Israel, was a divine punishment, not for sins of the sacred sphere, such as the wrong offering of sacrifice or other cultic errors, but for the social sins of the nation. The upper classes of Israelite society had oppressed the lower classes, and for this, they would be deprived of the leadership of the nation, which would become the possession of the Assyrians.

Now even if it was indeed because of such sins committed by Israelites against each other that YHWH was bringing the Assyrians, there was no realistic possibility that a restoration of right order to society would halt their advance. There is an element of *Realpolitik* in the message of Amos and all the eighth-century prophets. Once the Assyrians were mobilized, it was highly unlikely that they would be held back because the people of Israel "repented." Seen in this light, the "hopeless" interpretation of Amos, in which he is seen as saying that nothing will now prevent disaster, is surely more plausible than the alternative. The prophet did believe, however, that there was some point in getting the people he addressed to recognize that the invasion was the result of their own guilt, quite possibly because he thought that there might one day be a brighter dawn. People in dire situations often do believe such things, and religious people in horrible circumstances, in which they know that their doom is already sealed, may still look to God to bring good out of evil. But that is far from the same as thinking that a force like the Assyrians could be stopped in its tracks.

The God of Amos is a destroyer – a just destroyer, but a destroyer nonetheless. Although the prophet may look back to times when Yhwh had blessed Israel (if 3:2 is authentic), the immediate past in Amos's opinion has been a catalogue of disasters in which the divine hand can be seen warning the people of the consequences of their sin and foreshadowing the total destruction that is now on its way. Amos 4:6–11 is sometimes described as an *Unheilsgeschichte*, a history of devastation rather than a history of salvation, as one local problem after another is presented as Yhwh's attempt to get the people to take him seriously:[24]

> I gave you cleanness of teeth in all your cities,
>> and lack of bread in all your places,
> yet you did not return to me,
>>> says the Lord.
>
> And I also withheld the rain from you
>> when there were still three months to the harvest;
> I would send rain on one city
>> and no rain on another city;
> one field would be rained upon,
>> and the field on which it did not rain withered;
> so two or three towns wandered to one town
>> to drink water, and were not satisfied;
> yet you did not return to me,
>>> says the Lord.
>
> I struck you with blight and mildew;
>> I laid waste your gardens and your vineyards;
>> the locust devoured your fig trees and your olive trees;
> yet you did not return to me,
>>> says the Lord.

---

[24] Contrast the references to the history of salvation in 2:9–12, where the people are disobedient to Yhwh despite his acts of *grace* such as the exodus.

I sent among you a pestilence after the manner of Egypt;
>I killed your young men with the sword;
I carried away your horses;
>and I made the stench of your camp go up into your nostrils;
yet you did not return to me,

>>says the LORD.

I overthrew some of you,
>as when God overthrew Sodom and Gomorrah,
>and you were like a brand snatched from the fire;
yet you did not return to me,

>>says the LORD.

This unit reflects an attitude toward what we would now call natural disasters (blight, famine, disease) that was universal in the ancient world and very common in the recent past, and that is still prevalent in much of the world today, in which such afflictions are regarded as divine punishment for human sin. So Amos presupposes that his hearers will understand him when he describes them in precisely those terms. They have failed to take warning, but it is reasonable to think that they should have done so, according to the logic of his teaching. The idea of God here is well expressed in the "doxologies," even though they are probably a later addition to the words of Amos: YHWH is one who "makes the morning darkness" (4:13), turning joy into grief. YHWH's powers of destruction reach even into Sheol:

Though they dig into Sheol,
>from there shall my hand take them. (Amos 9:2)

even though it seems to have been widely believed that his power and authority did not extend to Sheol; and the sea serpent can be used by God as an instrument of punishment:

… though they hide from my sight at the bottom of the sea,
>there I will command the sea serpent, and it shall bite them.
(Amos 9:3)

Even the sea serpent, one of the surviving forces of chaos, is not a force outside Yʜwʜ's control. Even from the scope of Yʜwʜ's dark side, we see that he is in effect the God of a monotheistic system of thought. Amos does not mention or have room in his thinking for any other divinity, strongly suggesting that monotheism goes back into the eighth century even though it was almost certainly not a majority belief nor widely held at that time. The old description of the prophets as teaching "ethical monotheism" is thus not so far from the truth.

THE COVENANT

One of Amos's central beliefs is that Yʜwʜ's relationship with Israel is not unconditional. It is not simply that "Yʜwʜ is the God of Israel and Israel is the people of Yʜwʜ," or that Yʜwʜ is Israel's "helper." On the contrary, the continuation of the relationship depends on Israel's response, and because that response has been so direly inadequate, the relationship is about to end. In fact, the relationship is contractual rather than natural. Israel's privileged position as Yʜwʜ's people was a matter of choice on his part (3:2: "you only have I known of all the families of the earth"), and is maintained only as long as Israel keeps its side of the bargain. This is tantamount to saying that Amos believed in a covenant between Yʜwʜ and Israel, though it must be stressed that he never uses the word *bĕrît* (ברית), which in the eighth century appears to have been still only a political term meaning "treaty." Hosea is probably the first to apply the word metaphorically to the relationship between Yʜwʜ and Israel:

> But at Adam they transgressed the covenant;
> > there they dealt faithlessly with me. (Hos 6:7)

> Set the trumpet to your lips!
> > One like a vulture is over the house of the Lᴏʀᴅ,

> because they have broken my covenant
> and transgressed my law. (Hos 8:1)

The contractual character of the relationship between Yhwh and Israel does not appear to be one of the ideas that Amos could count on his hearers recognizing – which is why I did not include it among the religious beliefs current in eighth-century Israel, surveyed in the previous chapter. Instead, it seems to be an idea that Amos himself developed. There is, of course, a huge scholarly debate on the origins of the covenant and what it meant, which cannot be entered into here.[25] But in any case, it does not seem to be an idea Amos expects his audience to be familiar with, but is rather a new idea he is putting forward. It was commonly believed in Israel, as in other cultures of the ancient Near East, that the gods might avenge certain heinous sins (murder, rape, incest) on individuals and perhaps their families or clans, and infringements of cultic regulations could call forth divine wrath, but the thought that such things as having false balances or getting drunk would call down divine anger because they constituted a breach of some sort of contract between the gods and a nation had not, I believe, occurred to anyone prior to Amos. Leaders of a nation could put its status in jeopardy by failing to honor the gods – the relationship was to that extent contractual. But the contract did not include such matters as social relationships. There were laws about how people should relate in society, and there was a sense that the god was in a relationship with the nation as a whole, but no one had put these two ideas together to produce the covenant idea as we encounter it in Amos. It was, however, to prove a very rich concept

---

[25] See the important survey in Ernest W. Nicholson, *God and His People: Covenant and Theology in the Old Testament* (Oxford: Clarendon Press, 1986).

for the subsequent development of Israelite and Jewish theology.[26] Over the next few centuries, it was gradually codified within the developing book of Deuteronomy.

One of the things entailed by this notion of a Yhwh–Israel contract whose terms are the provisions of the legal code – and hence the rules about proper behavior toward other people, not simply the practices of the cult – is that transgressions of ethical norms by individuals, especially important and central individuals such as the ruling classes, endanger the whole life of the nation.[27] In looking for a reason for the impending destruction of Israel by the Assyrians, Amos hit upon the disordered state of Israelite society (as he saw it), with unjust inequalities between rich and poor, exploitation, oppression, excessive luxury – all the things that subsequent prophets would also identify as breaches of the covenant. The destruction would of course affect all equally, poor as much as rich, though it would probably be mainly the ruling classes who would be likely to experience exile, peasants being allowed to remain in the land and cope as best they could. But there would certainly be no fair discrimination between guilty and innocent such as is envisioned in the utopian ideas of Ezekiel, who believed that Yhwh distinguished the two groups and punished only the wicked.[28] For Amos, the whole country is affected – an entirely realistic picture of the result of invasion in ancient as in modern times.

---

[26] See Stanley E. Porter and Jacqueline C. R. de Roo, eds., *The Concept of Covenant in the Second Temple Period* (JSJSup 71; Leiden: Brill, 2003).

[27] See Heschel, *The Prophets*, esp. 17–19 ("Few Are Guilty, All Are Responsible").

[28] See, e.g., Ezekiel 9 and 18, but note that the corporate model still occurs in Ezekiel 21:4 ("I will cut off from you righteous and wicked"). For an extended treatment, see Jacqueline E. Lapsley, *Can These Bones Live? The Problem of the Moral Self in the Book of Ezekiel* (BZAW 301; Berlin: Walter de Gruyter, 2000).

For the modern reader, this is likely to seem unfair on Y<small>HWH</small>'s part, especially since it is the kind of conduct that would be condemned if it were carried out by a human being.[29] But Amos seems quite content with this way of seeing things. Y<small>HWH</small>'s justice is not diminished by the fact that he punishes the innocent along with the guilty or by the fact that he allows those who are already being oppressed by the rich and powerful to suffer again in the collapse of the nation when those same rich and powerful people are punished. The sense of group solidarity trumps the sense of unfairness. If the rulers have sinned, then it is "the nation" that has sinned. Plenty of people in the modern world still have beliefs of this kind, and in the ancient world it was quite normal to think that a ruler could be divinely punished by the gods killing his subjects – consider, for example, the story of David and the census in 2 Samuel 24. Such punishment amounted to robbing the ruler of his possessions, as that is what his subjects were, much as slaves were considered the property of their masters. But Amos tweaks this complex of ideas by adding that the moral infringements committed by the rulers include the way they behave toward these very subjects, and this introduces a note of paradox into the matter. Moreover, Amos also sees the infringements as not simply wrong, but as breaches of contract, and this seems to be an idea he was the first to have. It is quite interesting that even the later circles responsible for transmitting Amos's thoughts did not add the term "covenant," in the technical sense of a Y<small>HWH</small>–Israel contract, to the book, though, as we will see in the next chapter, the word does occur in Amos in a more secular sense.

---

[29] For thoughts on this, see Andrew Davies, *Double Standards in Isaiah: Re-evaluating Prophetic Ethics and Divine Justice* (BIS 46; Leiden: Brill, 2000).

CHAPTER 4

Theological Themes in the Additions to the Book of Amos

In accordance with the conclusions arrived at in Chapter 1, I will not treat the book of Amos as multilayered and having passed through many stages of redaction because, while this is entirely possible, it is also, I believe, impossible to prove. I will simply examine the various oracles identified as probably later additions, in order to assess their theological message. It seems to me that, despite the fact that they may span a considerable period of time, there is quite a coherent message in these additions, which differs at some points quite sharply from what we have been able to identify as the theology of Amos and his immediate circle. After this, I will go on in the next chapter to ask how, by being added to the earlier material, these additions change its meaning, and thus produce the synthetic theology of the *book* of Amos in its present form.

COVENANT

We ended the last chapter by looking at the covenant – never named as such by Amos, yet in all essentials probably one of his discoveries or inventions. Later editors had no reason to avoid the word *běrît* (ברית), which through the work of the authors of Deuteronomy and the deuteronomistic school, as seen in the historical books and in the book of Jeremiah, had become a central concept in Israel's thinking about the relationship between God and the nation. Even so, these redactors of Amos did not introduce the word into the book in its religious sense. *Bĕrît* is found, however, along with some associated ideas, in two of the oracles against the nations regarded by most scholars as secondary to the original core of five – specifically, the oracles against Tyre and Edom. The oracle against Tyre reads:

> Thus says the LORD:
> For three transgressions of Tyre,
>   and for four, I will not revoke the punishment;
> because they delivered entire communities over to Edom,
>   and did not remember the covenant of kinship.
> so I will send a fire on the wall of Tyre,
>   fire that shall devour its strongholds. (Amos 1:9–10)

It has not proved possible to identify with confidence the events this oracle refers to, and it is not certain that the "entire communities" handed over to Edom were Israelite. Like the (probably authentic) oracle against Moab, the text might be referring to offenses that did not involve Israelites at all (cf. Amos 2:1). But the general consensus is that it probably does refer to an offense against the Israelites proper, or more likely in fact against the Judeans, in a somewhat later period than the lifetime of Amos. The handing over of whole populations is said to offend against the "covenant of brothers" (NRSV: "covenant of kinship"), which almost certainly refers to the "brotherhood" between Israel and Edom, which in Genesis is symbolized by the fact that Esau and Jacob are literal, genetic brothers. The "covenant" here is not YHWH's covenant with his people but a treaty between Israel and Edom, and therefore the passage does not refer to "*the* covenant" at all in the theological sense.

The Edom oracle, which probably refers to the participation of Edomites in the sack of Jerusalem, which is also condemned in Obadiah, does not use the word *bĕrît*, but once again refers to Israel and Edom as brothers:

> Thus says the LORD:
> For three transgressions of Edom
>   And for four, I will not revoke the punishment;
> Because he pursued his brother with the sword
>   And cast off all pity;
> He maintained his anger perpetually,
>   And kept his wrath for ever.
> So I will send a fire on Teman,
>   And it shall devour the strongholds of Bozrah. (Amos 1:1–12)

The two oracles thus fit naturally together, and it seems quite likely that they were added at the same time. Both are simpler in structure than the authentic oracles against the nations, and both follow exactly the same pattern.

In the Edom oracle certainly, and in the Tyre oracle probably, we have a condemnation of a foreign nation for outrages committed against Israel. There is lacking the sense we find in the other oracles against the nations that atrocities in warfare are wrong in and of themselves. Rather, what Tyre and Edom have done wrong is to *attack Israel*. By the time these passages were added, the sense of Israel as YHWH's special people has reasserted itself – not, in all probability, that it had ever gone away. But the contrast with Amos himself is striking. These prophecies are nationalistic in a way that the authentic oracles against the nations are not. Would Amos have condemned the Edomites for helping with the sack of Jerusalem, if he could have been transported forward into the sixth century? We cannot say for certain, of course; but there seems a reasonable chance that he would have taken much the attitude that

Isaiah took toward the invasion of the Assyrians in 701 – namely, that the foreign nation was Yhwh's instrument of punishment on his own people:

> Ah, Assyria, the rod of my anger –
>> the club in their hands is my fury!
> Against a godless nation I send him,
>> and against the people of my wrath I command him,
> to take spoil and seize plunder,
>> and to tread them down like the mire of the streets. (Isa 10:5–6)

Such an idea is entirely foreign to whoever wrote Amos 1:9–15; in that person's perspective, to attack Israel (Judah) is to attack Yhwh himself.

TORAH

The other oracle among the oracles against the nations that is usually regarded as secondary is the one against Judah:

> Thus says the LORD:
> For three transgressions of Judah
>> and for four, I will not revoke the punishment;
> because they have rejected the law of the LORD,
>> and have not kept his statutes,
> but they have been led away by the same lies
>> after which their ancestors walked.
> so I will send a fire on Judah,
>> and it shall devour the strongholds of Jerusalem. (Amos 2:4–5)

As we saw in Chapter 1, since the work of W. H. Schmidt, it has been usual to treat this passage as part of the deuteronomistic edition of the book of Amos, probably carried out during the exile when other prophetic books were also being subjected to deuteronomistic editing – notably and especially, the book of Jeremiah.[1] Not all commentators have agreed that Amos 2:4–5 is deuteronomistic, but it does have two features that seem to put it in that ambit: (1) the condemnation of Judah for disobeying the law, and (2) the reference to the gods other than Yhwh whom they have worshipped as "lies." True, the word used here (*kāzāb*) hardly occurs elsewhere in the deuteronomistic corpus,[2] but the idea that a false god is a "lie" is very close to deuteronomistic thinking, though it may also owe something to the teaching of Isaiah or even Deutero-Isaiah (note Isa 44:20, where the idol maker should ask himself "Is not this thing in my right hand a fraud [Hebrew *šeqer*]?") – who in turn may have influenced the Deuteronomists. Whereas Amos had condemned the nations for war crimes, the author of this oracle fixes on disobedience to the law (*torah*) as the great sin of Judah. Amos nowhere else mentions the law at all, and the theoretical thinking behind this oracle is thus quite different from his. As we saw in the last chapter, Amos seems to condemn the people's misdemeanors as each wrong in itself, and there is no sign that he had an overarching ethical theory such as the idea of Torah found in later Jewish thought. What the upper classes have done wrong in oppressing the poor is like what the nations have done wrong in committing atrocities during war: offending against individual moral norms that ought to be self-evident. The mentality that condemns such things on the grounds that they form part of an official legal code,

---

[1] W. H. Schmidt, "Die deuteronomistische Redaktion des Amosbuches: Zu den theologischen Unterschieden zwischen dem Prophetenwort und seinem Sammler," *ZAW* 77 (1965): 168–192.

[2] In fact, only at Judges 16:10, 13, where it has the ordinary meaning "lie" – namely, the lie that Samson told Delilah.

linked to the covenant, does not seem to have played a part in the prophet Amos's thinking.

Such an idea did become very prevalent through the work of the deuteronomistic school, however, and we can see it in the book of Jeremiah and of course in the Deuteronomistic History:

> Thus says the LORD, the God of Israel: Cursed be anyone who does not heed the words of this covenant, which I commanded your ancestors when I brought them out of the land of Egypt, from the iron-smelter, saying, Listen to my voice, and do all that I command you. (Jer 11:3–4)

> And when you tell this people all these words, and they say to you, "Why has the LORD pronounced all this great evil against us? What is our iniquity? What is the sin that we have committed against the LORD our God?" then you shall say to them: It is because your ancestors have forsaken me, says the LORD, and have gone after other gods and have served and worshipped them, and have forsaken me and have not kept my law. (Jer 16:10–11)

> In this house and in Jerusalem, which I have chosen out of all the tribes of Israel, I will put my name for ever; I will not cause the feet of Israel to wander any more out of the land that I gave to their ancestors, if only they will be careful to do according to all that I have commanded them, and according to all the law that my servant Moses commanded them. (2 Kgs 21:7–8)

If we follow the Göttingen School's stratification of the Deuteronomistic History, then the layer that speaks of observance of the law is the one they dub DtrN (the "nomistic" or legal stratum), coming from a time toward the end of the exile and thus more or less contemporary with Deutero-Isaiah.[3] It seems to me

---

3   See Rudolf Smend, *Die Entstehung des Alten Testaments* (Stuttgart, Berlin, Mainz: Kohlhammer, 1981); Timo Veijola, *Das Königtum in der Beurteilung der deuteronomistischen Historiographie: Eine redaktionsgeschichtliche Untersuchung* (Helsinki: Suomalainen Tiedeakatemia, 1977); idem, *Die ewige Dynastie: David und die Entstehung seiner Dynastie nach der*

that this is probably the period from which Amos's Judah oracle also derives. This period may also have produced the great oracle about the Torah streaming out from Jerusalem found in Isaiah 2 and Micah 4:

> In days to come
>> the mountain of the LORD's house
> shall be established as the highest of the mountains,
>> and shall be raised above the hills;
> all the nations shall stream to it.
>> Many peoples shall come and say,
> "Come, let us go up to the mountain of the LORD,
>> to the house of the God of Jacob;
> that he may teach us his ways
>> and that we may walk in his paths."
> For out of Zion shall go forth instruction [*torah*],
>> and the word of the LORD from Jerusalem.
>> > (Isa 2:2–3; cf. Micah 4:1–2)

PROPHECY

Whatever the case, the idea of prophecy that lies behind the Judah oracle in Amos 2:4–5 is quite different from that of Amos himself. The prophet here is one who tries to keep Israel/Judah on track in its observance of the law, rather like the "prophet like Moses" of Deuteronomy 18:15. This is part of the image of the prophet as a "helpful" figure – calling the people to order and trying to win them back to the Torah – which belongs to a time period later than Amos, to a time when the notion of prophecy as a continuing institution in Israel had emerged. In biblical scholarship of

deuteronomistischen Darstellung (Helsinki: Suomalainen Tiedeakatemia, 1975); and Walter Dietrich, *Prophetie und Geschichte: Eine redaktionsgeschichtliche Untersuchung zum deuteronomistischen Geschichtswerk* (FRLANT 108; Göttingen: Vandenhoeck & Ruprecht, 1972).

the mid-twentieth century, it was thought that this indeed had been the role of the prophets, who were thus seen as "covenant-mediators" of a sort. R. E. Clements, in his influential *Prophecy and Covenant,* followed a common mid-century perspective in seeing the prophets as those charged with transmitting the covenant from generation to generation and encouraging the people to keep it by proper observance of the laws and ordinances that went with it.[4] What I have presented in this study as a novel creation of Amos – namely, that the relationship between YHWH and Israel was essentially contractual – scholars of the mid-twentieth century tended to think of as an immemorial idea that might even go back to Moses, which is of course how the Old Testament itself presents matters. The great prophets were thus seen as not dissimilar from the prophets of court and sanctuary, religious functionaries whose task was to keep the people loyal to YHWH by teaching his Torah.

These ideas waned as the twentieth century drew to a close, and most would now probably not think of the prophets as having had this role, in part because the covenant is no longer generally seen as so old, and the prophets are once again thought of as more innovators than traditionalists. Be that as it may, it is clear that whoever wrote Amos 2:4–5 did have some such notion of the prophetic task in mind. Amos 3:7 accords with this idea of prophets:

> Surely the Lord GOD does nothing,
>   without revealing his secret
>   to his servants the prophets.

As we have seen, this does not fit its present context, which consists of a series of sayings about cause and effect, arguing that from

---

4 R. E. Clements, *Prophecy and Covenant* (London: SCM, 1965); subsequently much modified in idem, *Prophecy and Tradition* (Oxford: Blackwell, 1975).

various observable events one can reason back to their cause. But in 3:7, we have an assertion that nothing significant happens without its being predicted, which is an entirely different point. Its interpolation seeks to establish that YHWH never brings about important events without foretelling them, and so encourages the reader to take Amos's words as just such an authoritative prediction. The phrase "his servants the prophets" is particularly striking, presenting as it does the prophets as standing in a long line – very much in line with the idea of the "prophet like Moses." The picture of Israel's history that is presupposed here is essentially that of the Deuteronomistic History, in which a "prophecy and fulfilment" scheme serves as the structuring principle, as Gerhard von Rad showed.[5] Throughout that corpus, prophets arise at salient moments in the history of the nation to warn of coming events, sometimes many generations before they occur – the most spectacular example being the fate of Jericho:

> Joshua then pronounced this oath, saying,
> "Cursed before the LORD be anyone who tries
> to build this city – this Jericho!
> At the cost of his firstborn he shall lay its foundation,
> And at the cost of his youngest he shall set up its gates!"
> (Josh 6:26)

> In his [i.e., Ahab's] days Hiel of Bethel built Jericho; he laid its foundation at the cost of Abiram his firstborn, and set up its gates at the cost of his youngest son Segub, according to the word of the LORD, which he spoke by Joshua son of Nun. (1 Kgs 16:34)

The Deuteronomistic History can very reasonably be called a prophetic history – well captured by its Jewish title the "Former

---

5 Gerhard von Rad, "The Deuteronomic Theology of History in *I* and *II Kings*," in idem, *The Problem of the Hexateuch and Other Essays* (trans. E. W. Trueman Dicken; Edinburgh: Oliver and Boyd, 1966), 205–221.

Prophets" – in which prophetic interventions keep happening and prophets are clearly a national institution. This contrasts sharply with the presentation of Amos in 7:10–17 as denying that he is a prophet, or at least denying that he is part of the prophetic institution. He is willing to use the verb "prophesy" for his own activity, but apparently not the noun "prophet," and this strongly suggests that the title implied for him an undesirable, possibly dubiously orthodox kind of religious functionary, just as it did later for Jeremiah:

> In the prophets of Samaria
>> I saw a disgusting thing:
> they prophesied by Baal
>> and led my people Israel astray.
> But in the prophets of Jerusalem
>> I have seen a more shocking thing:
> they commit adultery and walk in lies;
>> they strengthen the hands of evildoers,
>> so that no one turns from wickedness;
> all of them have become like Sodom to me,
>> and its inhabitants like Gomorrah.
> Therefore thus says the LORD of hosts concerning the prophets:
> "I am going to make them eat wormwood,
>> and give them poisoned water to drink;
> for from the prophets of Jerusalem
>> ungodliness has spread throughout the land." (Jer 23:13–15)

> I did not send the prophets,
>> yet they ran;
> I did not speak to them,
>> yet they prophesied.
> But if they had stood in my council,
>> then they would have proclaimed my words to my people,
> and they would have turned them from their evil way,
>> and from the evil of their doings. (Jer 23:21–22)

But for the author of Amos 3:7, the word "prophet" has no such undesirable associations, and designates someone in a line of succession, unequivocally authorized by Yʜwʜ, whose job it is to keep Israel informed of salient coming events. This is thus a deuteronomistic rather than an "Amosean" image of prophecy. It is also found in 2:11, where Yʜwʜ "raised up some of your children to be prophets."

IDOLATRY

The additional material in Amos also includes two condemnations of idolatry, in 5:26–27 and 8:14. I treat these in order:

> You shall take up Sakkuth your king, and Kaiwan your star-god, your images that you made for yourselves; therefore I will take you into exile beyond Damascus, says the Lᴏʀᴅ, whose name is the God of hosts. (Amos 5:26–27)

It is not clear in this text whether the worship of other gods is the sin the people have committed or if it is being said that when they go into exile they will have to take their "images" with them. The lack of clarity is due to the verb, since it is not certain if it should be understood as past or future in orientation. In either case, the gods are said to be things "you made for yourselves," which is how idols are described in the book of Isaiah:

> Their land is filled with idols;
> > they bow down to the work of their hands,
> > to what their own fingers have made. (Isa 2:8)

Given that Isaiah may have spoken in these terms in Judah in the eighth century (assuming the relevant passages are not interpolations there too!), it is possible that Amos could also have uttered these words. But generally his condemnations in the cultic sphere seem to be about the wrong way of *worshipping Yʜwʜ* – through sacrifice rather than social justice – and not about the worship of other gods. As we have already seen, Amos 2:4, which condemns "lies," that is, false gods, is a later addition. Regardless, the theology here is certainly interesting because it represents a very "advanced" way of understanding images used in worship as mere fabricated objects, a theme that was to become part of the rhetoric of Jewish derision of idolatry in Jeremiah, in Deutero-Isaiah, and in later texts:

> They are both stupid and foolish;
> > the instruction given by idols is no better than wood!
> Beaten silver is brought from Tarshish,
> > and gold from Uphaz.
> They are the work of the artisan and of the hands of the goldsmith;
> > their clothing is blue and purple;
> > they are all the product of skilled workers. (Jer 10:8–9)

> Those who lavish gold from the purse,
> > and weigh out silver in the scales –
> they hire a goldsmith, who makes it into a god;
> > then they fall down and worship!
> They lift it to their shoulders, they carry it,
> > they set it in its place, and it stands there;
> > it cannot move from its place.
> If one cries out to it, it does not answer,
> > or save anyone from trouble. (Isa 46:6–7)

> So the king said to him, "Why do you not worship Bel?" He answered, "Because I do not revere idols made with hands, but the living God, who created heaven and earth and has dominion over all living creatures."
> > The king said to him again, "Do you not think Bel is a living god? Do you not see how much he eats and drinks every day?" And Daniel laughed, and said, "Do not be deceived, O king, for this thing is only clay inside and bronze outside, and it never ate or drank anything." (Bel and the Dragon 4a-7)

In later Judaism, this "idol-polemic" was carried through very consistently.[6] From an outsider's perspective, the polemic would

---

[6] Against the argument that Amos 5:26–27 must be late, we might think that something like this argument already occurs in Hosea: "My people consult a piece of

certainly have been judged unfair. People in ancient times did not simply nor simplistically identify the god with the image, but saw the image as a place in which the power and aura of the god was concentrated.[7] A fairer comparison is perhaps with the icons used in Orthodox Christian worship, or with articles such as crucifixes in Roman Catholicism. These are reverenced by worshippers, but not because they are thought to be divine in themselves, out of context. The insistence that the image *is* the god is a tendentious interpretation designed to ridicule gods other than Yʜwʜ. Nevertheless, it cannot be denied that the aniconic nature of Israel's worship expresses a powerful message about the absoluteness and freedom of its God. In later times, pagan philosophers were impressed by the imageless worship of the Jews, and within Christianity there have been periodic reassertions of this style of worship, in the iconoclast controversy in the Orthodox Church and in the Protestant Reformation. Whether or not images should be used in worship, the point that the refusal of them makes is an important one about the non-comparability of God with any physical thing and thus God's absolute independence from human worshippers. And it may be doubted whether Jewish monotheism would ever have been solidly established without the scorn of "idols" expressed through passages such as Amos 5:26.

We turn now to the other passage about "other gods":

> Those who swear by Ashimah of Samaria,
>   and say, "As your god lives, O Dan"

---

wood, and their divining-rod gives them oracles" (Hos 4:12). But this is really about the use of technical aids to divination rather than "idols." Hosea 13:2 does contain the argument: "And now they keep on sinning and make a cast image for themselves, idols of silver made according to their understanding, all of them the work of artisans." But most commentators think this is a later insertion in Hosea.

7   See Michael B. Dick, ed., *Born in Heaven, Made on Earth: The Making of the Cult Image in the Ancient Near East* (Winona Lake: Eisenbrauns, 1999).

and, "As the way of Beer-sheba lives" –
> they shall fall, and never rise again. (Amos 8:14)

The "false gods" are located in Samaria and Dan as well as Beersheba, which may suggest a preexilic origin for this oracle, so that again it could be by Amos or his circle. But general opinion is that this verse is a fragment from a later period, condemning the taking of oaths in the name of gods other than YHWH. The issue here then is not "idolatry" proper but disloyalty to YHWH, very much as in Amos's contemporary Hosea, where the worship of non-Yahwistic deities is the central complaint against the northern kingdom:

> The inhabitants of Samaria tremble
> > for the calf of Beth-aven.
> Its people shall mourn for it,
> > and its idolatrous priests shall wail over it,
> > over its glory that has departed from it.
> The thing itself shall be carried to Assyria
> > as tribute to the great king.
> Ephraim shall be put to shame,
> > and Israel shall be ashamed of his idol. (Hos 10:5–6)

> When Ephraim spoke, there was trembling;
> > he was exalted in Israel;
> > but he incurred guilt through Baal and died. (Hos 13:1)

It is one of the main contrasts between Hosea and Amos that the latter is not concerned with this issue.

JUDGMENT

The oracle in Amos 8:11–12 is rather puzzling:

> The time is surely coming, says the Lord GOD,
> > When I will send a famine on the land;
> Not a famine of bread, or a thirst for water,
> > But of hearing the words of the LORD.

> They shall wander from sea to sea,
> > And from north to east;
> They shall run to and fro, seeking the word of the LORD,
> > But they shall not find it.

Amos surely foresaw a time of *literal* hardship for Israel, not a *metaphorical* famine of hearing the word of YHWH. This oracle thus belongs to a time when the prophetic message was being interpreted more "spiritually," with a concern for the religious rather than the physical well-being of the nation. It foresees a time when "visions were not widespread" (1 Sam 3:2) and people would wish to get in touch with YHWH but be unable to. This may reflect the postexilic belief in the end of prophecy, found in Zechariah 13:2–6 and often commented on in rabbinic literature.[8] For the rabbis, the deficit had been made good through the codification of the Torah, and, in addition, God still communicated through the *bat-qol*, a kind of echo of older prophecy. But there does seem to have been a period when the end of prophecy was mourned and people in Israel felt that God was no longer in touch with them as he had been of old. We may speculate that it was at some point during the Persian period, maybe in the fourth century, that this idea took root. If so, then perhaps this oracle comes from the same period. Theologically it bears witness to a sense that there had been a kind of golden age when YHWH and Israel were in intimate contact, whereas now the situation was more like a famine or a drought, with no access to divine communications. Given that the passage is couched in future terms, it is conceivable that Amos foresaw such an age, but his perspective is usually shorter than this and he makes predictions about

---

[8] See my discussion in John Barton, *Oracles of God: Perceptions of Ancient Prophecy in Israel after the Exile* (2nd ed.; New York: Oxford University Press, 2007 [1st ed.: 1986]), 105–116.

the immediate rather than the more remote future. The idea that God might withdraw from contact with his chosen nation is, however, certainly reminiscent of Amos. Hence, this is the kind of secondary oracle that, even if quite late, shows a real understanding of the prophet's thought.

THE REMNANT

We come now to the closing oracles in the book that touch on a number of themes common in later prophecy. The prophecies of Amos as collected soon after his death ended, it seems, with 9:8ab:

> The eyes of the Lord GOD are upon the sinful kingdom,
> And I will destroy it from the face of the earth.

It was a later glossator who rather crudely added the final line, 9:8c:

> – except that I will not utterly destroy the house of Jacob,
> says the LORD.

This addition ruins the effect of finality and reflects the later awareness that Israel (Judah) had not in fact totally perished – and since Amos must have been right, according to later perceptions of prophetic accuracy or veracity, he must have predicted a less-than-complete collapse. The gloss is thus a clear indication of a later theology, in which God has a plan to punish but not to destroy Israel – a judgment that refines and purges but does not annihilate, very much like Isaiah 1:25–26:

> I will turn my hand against you;
> I will smelt away your dross as with lye
> and remove all your alloy.
> And I will restore your judges as at the first,
> and your counsellors as at the beginning.
> Afterwards you shall be called the city of righteousness,
> the faithful city.

A related theme is that of the discriminating judgment: Israel will be sieved or sifted in such a way that God will distinguish between the righteous and the wicked, and only the latter will be destroyed:

> For lo, I will command
>   and shake the house of Israel among all the nations
> as one shakes with a sieve,
>   but no pebble shall fall to the ground.
> All the sinners of my people shall die by the sword,
>   who say, "Evil shall not overtake or meet us." (Amos 9:9–10)

The general consensus has been that this idea began with Ezekiel, who in chapter 9 presents a tableau or allegory in which a group of men go through Jerusalem to kill the wicked and are accompanied by a scribe whose task is to mark (with a letter *tāw*, which in Palaeo-Hebrew is a cross or x-shape) the foreheads of the righteous, "those who sigh and groan over all the abominations that are committed" in the city (Ezek 9:4). In practice, the disaster of the exile, which Ezekiel is here predicting, did not discriminate between good and bad people, and, indeed, he does not say that the scribe actually found anyone to mark. Perhaps the point of the vision is simply to indicate that God was not unjust: if he had found any righteous people, he would have spared them (cf. Gen 18:16–33). Indeed, later on in Ezekiel, any "remnant" that may be left after the destruction is not a sign that there were good people in the city but rather that there were some so wicked that God left them alive as a kind of terrible visual aid of just how bad things had become:

> Yet, survivors shall be left in it [Jerusalem], sons and daughters who will be brought out. When you see their ways and their deeds, you will be consoled for the evil that I have brought upon Jerusalem.

> They shall console you, when you see their ways and their deeds;
> and you shall know that it was not without cause that I did all that I
> have done in it, says the Lord GOD. (Ezek 14:22–23; cf. 12:16)

Nevertheless, further on in the book, we do find the idea of a discriminating judgment that will leave a remnant:

> I will purge out the rebels among you, and those who transgress
> against me; I will bring them out of the land where they reside as
> aliens. (Ezek 20:38)

This may be an addition to Ezekiel, but it is certainly in his spirit. The theological basis is provided by the discussion in Ezekiel 18, where the prophet insists that YHWH never transfers guilt from one person or generation to another. Those who suffer are always the sinners – no one suffers for the sins of another. This appears to run contrary to Amos's belief that the coming judgment would fall on the whole nation, on those culpable and on those not culpable but who would be caught up in the general destruction nevertheless. Amos's ideas here are much more true to the facts on the ground: no ancient invasion distinguished between good and bad as a country was overrun, and it was far from plausible to suggest that God would ensure that everyone who was killed was one of the sinners. Ezekiel's theory is a piece of speculation unrelated to the reality of ancient warfare, indeed a piece of "dogma" in the popular and negative sense of that word – a statement that is adhered to in defiance of the facts. Discriminating judgments are what human beings would like God to bring about, but seem rarely if ever to occur in practice. Note, by the way, that one of the things that constitutes the wickedness of the "sinners of my people" in Amos 9:10 is that they are blasé about the possibility of punishment, which is very Amos-like – compare Amos 6:6: "those who are not grieved over the ruin of Joseph." This fragment could thus well be a genuine reminiscence of Amos himself, since complacency and self-satisfaction are here the great sins, as often in both Amos and Isaiah:

> Alas for those who are at ease in Zion,[9]
>> and for those who feel secure on Mount Samaria. (Amos 6:1)

> Ah, the proud garland of the drunkards of Ephraim,
>> and the fading flower of its glorious beauty,
>> which is on the head of those bloated with rich food, of
>>> those overcome with wine. (Isa 28:1)

THE HOUSE OF DAVID

The prediction of the restoration of the house of David in 9:11–12 belongs to a widespread postexilic hope for a new king, a line of thought that eventually results in the messianism of later times, where a king of David's line gradually takes on more supernatural characteristics (see especially Jeremiah 30–34):

> On that day I will raise up
>> the booth of David that is fallen,
> and repair its breaches
>> and raise up its ruins,
>> and rebuild it as in the days of old,
> in order that they may possess the remnant of Edom
>> and all the nations who are called by my name,
>> says the LORD who does this. (Amos 9:11–12)

Here, the hope is evidently for an actual new king who will restore the "empire" David was believed to have ruled, including the surrounding states such as Edom, which is here singled out for mention again, perhaps because it had become such a notable

---

9 The phrase "in Zion" may suggest that this is an addition to the words of Amos if he was concerned only with the North.

enemy of Judah during the sack of Jerusalem in 587 (cf. Joel 3:19 [Hebrew 4:19], where Edom will become "a desolate wilderness"). The nearest parallel to this oracle is, probably significantly, found in Obadiah, where other states become the possession of various tribes and areas of the restored Israel, and Edom ("Mount Esau") is to be ruled directly by Israel, just as in Amos 9:12:

> Those of the Negeb shall possess Mount Esau,
> and those of the Shephelah the land of the Philistines;
> they shall possess the land of Ephraim and the land of Samaris,
> and Benjamin shall possess Gilead.
> The exiles of Israel who are in Halah
> shall possess Phoenicia as far as Zarephath;
> and the exiles of Jerusalem who are in Sepharad
> shall possess the towns of the Negeb.
> Those who have been saved shall go up to Mount Zion
> to rule Mount Esau,
> and the kingdom shall be the LORD's. (Obad 19–21)

Thus the area Edom had formerly occupied becomes Israel's. The oracle in Amos 9:11–12 makes no sense at all in the time of Amos, but it fits easily into postexilic Yehud, where there was a constant hope that what had now become a very small and dependent state would one day rise from the ashes and become again the heart of a world empire, a vision to which Obadiah bears eloquent witness. We find the notion also in Micah 7:14–17 and in Zephaniah 3:16–20:

> Shepherd your people with your staff,
> the flock that belongs to you,
> which lives alone in a forest
> in the midst of a garden land;
> let them feed in Bashan and Gilead
> as in the days of old.
> As in the days when you came out of the land of Egypt,
> show us marvellous things.

The nations shall see and be ashamed of all their might;
they shall lay their hands on their mouths;
    their ears shall be deaf;
they shall lick dust like a snake,
    like the crawling things of the earth;
they shall come trembling out of their fortresses;
    they shall turn in dread to the LORD our God,
    and they shall stand in fear of you. (Micah 7:14–17)

On that day it shall be said to Jerusalem:
Do not fear, O Zion,
    do not let your hands grow weak.
The LORD, your God, is in your midst,
    a warrior who gives victory;
he will rejoice over you with gladness,
    he will renew you in his love;
he will exult over you with loud singing
    as on a day of festival.
I will remove disaster from you,
    so that you will not bear reproach for it.
I will deal with all your oppressors at that time.
And I will save the lame
    and gather the outcast,
and I will change their shame into praise
    and renown in all the earth.
At that time I will bring you home,
    at the time when I gather you;
for I will make you renowned and praised
    among all the peoples of the earth,
when I restore your fortunes
    before your eyes, says the LORD. (Zeph 3:16–20)

The hopes of postexilic times were very unrealistic in the sense that they were highly unlikely to be fulfilled, but they were "realistic" in the sense that they were couched in terms of international political relations, rather than being concerned with "a new heaven and a new earth" as in Revelation 21:1. They were "this-worldly."

THE TRANSFORMATION OF NATURE

The final oracle in the book of Amos moves out of political reality into the realm of the transformation of nature, and this is a somewhat less common theme of postexilic prophecy, though we do find it in Trito-Isaiah and Zechariah. The former is the actual source of the phrase "new heaven and new earth," but it seems that what is envisioned is actually a rejuvenated and improved earth rather than a replacement one:

> For I am about to create new heavens
>> and a new earth;
> the former things shall not be remembered
>> or come to mind.
> But be glad and rejoice for ever
>> in what I am creating;
> for I am about to create Jerusalem as a joy,
>> and its people as a delight.
> I will rejoice in Jerusalem,
>> and delight in my people;
> no more shall the sound of weeping be heard in it,
>> or the cry of distress.
> No more shall there be in it
>> an infant that lives but a few days,
>> or an old person who does not live out a lifetime;
> for one who dies at a hundred years will be counted a youth,
>> and one who falls short of a hundred
>>> will be considered accursed.
> They shall build houses and inhabit them;
>>> they shall plant vineyards and eat their fruit.
> They shall not build and another inhabit;
>> they shall not plant and another eat;
> for like the days of a tree shall the days of my people be,
>> and my chosen shall long enjoy the work of their hands.
> They shall not labour in vain,
>> or bear children for calamity;
> for they shall be offspring blessed by the LORD –
>> and their descendants as well.

Before they call I will answer,
>   while they are yet speaking I will hear.
The wolf and the lamb shall feed together,
>   the lion shall eat straw like the ox;
>   but the serpent – its food shall be dust!
They shall not hurt or destroy
>   on all my holy mountain,
>>>   says the LORD. (Isa 65:17–25)

But now I will not deal with the remnant of this people as in the former days, says the LORD of hosts. For there shall be a sowing of peace; the vine shall yield its fruit, the ground shall give its produce, and the skies shall give their dew; and I will cause the remnant of this people to possess all these things. (Zech 8:11–12)

So also in the final oracle in the book of Amos: not only the human but also the natural world reflects the glorious future YHWH has in store for his chosen people, who will have more crops than they know what to do with, and more crops than they can successfully harvest:

The time is surely coming, says the LORD,
>   when the one who ploughs shall overtake the one who reaps,
>   and the treader of grapes the one who sows the seed;
The mountains shall drip sweet wine,
>   and all the hills shall flow with it.
I will restore the fortunes of my people Israel,
>   and they shall rebuild the ruined cities and inhabit them;
they shall plant vineyards and drink their wine,
>   and they shall make gardens and eat their fruit.
I will plant them upon their land,
>   and they shall never again be plucked up
>   out of the land that I have given them,
>>>   says the LORD your God. (Amos 9:13–15)

It is never easy to tell how literally such passages are meant to be taken. Presumably, whoever wrote this one did not actually imagine that the plower would literally overtake the reaper – this is simply a way of stressing the enormous yield of the crops. But did the author in fact believe that the crops would be miraculously improved anyway? Probably he thought in terms of guaranteed fruitfulness, such that there would be plenty and to spare. What is clear is that we are here moving beyond the political sphere in which the preexilic prophets were interested, and into one centered more on nature; though it is worth remembering that Amos himself, or his disciples, already taught that the *failure* of crops could be traced back to the hand of YHWH, who had used this to try to warn his people of the threat hanging over them (Amos 4:9).

To be sure, the dividing line between the world of politics and the world of nature is far from being so sharp in the Old Testament as it is in modern thinking, and events in one can have an impact on the other. The gods gave portents in heaven and earth before great political events; equally, great political restorations could go hand in hand with a transformation of nature. But that does not mean the oracle in Amos 9 is likely to be authentic. Amos saw a bleak future, with just a hint of possible survivors; he did not foretell wonders of agricultural abundance.

CONCLUSION

We could synthesize the theology of the additions to Amos along the following lines. Prophecy has long existed as an institution within Israel, and it goes back to the earliest days, after the exodus. Its purpose is to keep the people faithful to the worship of the one God and his laws by teaching and preaching, but in practice, the people have often been disobedient. The result of failure to remain faithful is divine punishment, but in this, the wicked suffer while the righteous remain safe. Persistent disobedience may result in the downfall of national institutions such as the monarchy, but YHWH is faithful to his promises and will renew the purified nation. He has in store a future of amazing fruitfulness for the restored land. Nations that oppose Israel will be punished for this crime. The idea of YHWH that lies behind this story of the role of prophecy in the history of Israel is that YHWH is above all both a righteous and a purposeful God. He does not act at random but according to a set purpose, and he always foretells what he is about to do, so that people have no excuse for disobedience and cannot say that they had not been warned. He is also not vindictive: beyond judgment there is help and redemption, and, after all its tribulations, Israel (meaning by this a new nation shaped around the remnant of the righteous) will enjoy divine blessings into an indefinite future. Thus the ethos of the additions to Amos is upbeat and positive.

I would argue that this theology is far removed from that of Amos of Tekoa, who does not think in terms of this kind of theological "package" but has a much more angular message, prompted by far more immediate concerns, arising either out of the Aramean war or from an awareness of the distant rumbling of Assyria beginning to prepare for western adventures. The idea of a codified set of laws is alien to him – he thinks more in terms of specific moral obligations, each of which is justified by its inherent rightness rather than because it stands in a body of authorized legal material such as the Torah became in later Judaism. His perspective probably barely involved the southern kingdom and certainly did not envision its collapse and later renewal. For him, one of the most appalling aspects of the sins of the ruling classes was precisely that, in the judgment they were bringing about, there could be no discrimination between those deserving and those undeserving of punishment; instead, the entire nation would perish, including the very people who were already suffering through the depredations of the powerful. This is a wholly unappealing but entirely realistic prediction. By contrast, the authors of the additions to the book lived in a more theoretical world in which divine judgment could be finely tuned to distinguish good people from bad. The wicked, for these authors, were not those who oppressed the poor so much as those who disobeyed the Torah or were disloyal to Yhwh through idolatry, together with other nations who opposed Yhwh's people – each of which are important themes in later prophets and in many other parts of the Old Testament, but which are not present in the teaching of Amos himself.

A central aspect of all this is the resurgence of an eschatology of salvation for Israel, which, as we saw, seems to have characterized the thinking of Amos's audience but which he himself had tried to suppress. It returns in full force in the thought of those who added to his book. The "day of Yhwh" for them would turn out to be light rather than darkness after all, just as Amos's audience had thought, though in fairness it must be said that the light lies on the other side of darkness, not as a substitute for it. Those who added to Amos shared the prophet's own moral seriousness, but they were ultimately optimists. Since they lived on the other side of the searing experience of the exile, they felt with some justification that things would never be as bad again as they had been in the past, and they therefore looked forward to better days. Where theodicy for Amos was a matter of accepting the terrible fate that awaited the nation as a just punishment for almost infinite guilt, for them it meant the exact apportionment of punishment to responsibility, in such a way that only the wicked would ever suffer, while the righteous were spared to become the nucleus of a new people of Yhwh. There was no doubt in their minds that they themselves formed part of this nucleus – for they were still alive, after the worst that the Babylonians could throw at them and their forebears. This was the clearest possible sign that they were the elect, the people with whom Yhwh had made his covenant and to whom he would be eternally faithful.

CHAPTER 5

The Theology of the Book of Amos

Can there be a theology of the finished book of Amos? Does the book, as opposed to its constituent parts, have any coherence? The underlying supposition of the Old Testament Theology series in which the present book is appearing is obviously that there can be such a theology. But this was not always self-evident to earlier generations of modern critical biblical scholars, who tended to think that coherence could be found only by removing ("deleting") the later additions that we looked at in the preceding chapter, so as to arrive at the theology of the prophet Amos himself. By now, the reader will have realized that I have some sympathy with that belief. I do think that the attempt to get back to the prophet himself is worthwhile and important. On the other hand, there is a *book* of Amos, and it contains the additions as well as the original words of the prophet, and in modern times it has become normal to think that it is possible to interpret the finished books of the Bible as well as their original cores. Indeed, some scholars now think that the final form of the book has a greater claim on our attention than do the hypothetical earlier stages.

THREE APPROACHES TO THE FINAL FORM

We can identify three different though related routes to a "final form" reading of any biblical book, and this is certainly the case for the book of Amos.

1. The first still belongs in the world of "historical criticism," and is traditionally called "redaction criticism" or now, sometimes, "composition criticism." This is the study of how the various component parts of a biblical book, acknowledged to have had disparate origins, became combined to form the finished whole. The term "composition criticism" tends to refer less to independent source materials that have been woven together – as in the traditional critical evaluation of the production of the Pentateuch by a final redactor (R) – and more to the gradual supplementation of an existing text by scribes who wrote additional material into it, a process called in German *Fortschreibung*. There is no accepted English term for this: "continuation" is about the best English has to offer. Whatever the case, the term describes the scribal activity that in Pentateuchal studies underlay the old "supplementary hypothesis," in which material was added to an existing core rather than being amalgamated from several discrete sources. Whether this really happened in the case of the Pentateuch is uncertain, but where the prophets are concerned it may very well be near the truth.

In other words, the editors of Amos may not have had the words of Amos plus collections of other sayings, which they then combined, but rather may have had the words of Amos and then added to them. This is more plausible for some parts of the book than others. For example, the "doxologies" appear to be an originally independent text that was broken up and placed at three salient points in the book, whereas the epilogue (or parts of it) may have been added from scratch to the existing book. It is very hard to tell which process went on where, and it is entirely possible that we should reckon with both redaction, in the traditional sense of weaving disparate material together, and composition, in the sense of the addition of freely composed extra oracles to supplement what already existed (*Fortschreibung*).

Redaction and composition criticism together imply that there was a deliberate attempt to give the book a new slant by the addition of "inauthentic" material, and exegetical skill is thus needed to interpret the final product in relation to the meaning of the earlier stages. The task is complex but not impossible, though the more minute the analysis, the harder it is to be confident that the exegesis is correct. Any hypothesis that a scribe has given a whole passage a new twist by adding a fraction of a verse is bound to be hard to verify, however reasonable it is in principle.

2. A second "holistic" approach to biblical books ignores questions of authorial or redactional intention and asks simply about the effect made by the text in its final form. This approach is indebted to modern literary criticism outside biblical studies, in which there is often an antipathy to the work of literary reconstruction of earlier versions or sources of texts and a preference for the text as it lies before us. In Shakespeare studies, for example, such an approach would not be interested in the way the text of the plays changed from early acting drafts to the (various) final printed editions, but would simply take one version of a play and interpret that as it stands.

The normal term for this kind of interpretation is "synchronic," that is, the interpretation of a text as it exists at one moment in time, rather than "diachronic," the study of the text through different points in time. Synchronic reading is not interested in textual criticism, or the various forms of "higher" criticism such as source and form criticism, but only in the text as it confronts us now. It asks not what J or E or P meant but rather what Genesis or Exodus or the Pentateuch as a whole means. In the case of a prophetic text, synchronic study ignores what may have been intended by the "real" Amos or by the authors of the various additions to his words, and concentrates instead on a straightforward reading of the finished book. Inconsistencies and contradictions, such as those that lead historical critics to hypothesize about sources and editions, become evidence of the self-contradictory nature of the finished text, or else are smoothed out by being seen as two sides of a single coin. Literary readings of the text in this mode are not interested in how the text came to be, but only in how it now is. Meaning may be conveyed through literary structure as well as through overt statements in the book, but this structure is not necessarily attributed to the intentions of a redactor. For all we know, it may sometimes be the result of chance or accident. The important point is that it is there in the text as we now encounter it.

3. Finally, the last fifty years have seen the growth of a consciously theological justification for concentrating on the final form of biblical texts, in the rise of the so-called "canonical approach" developed by Brevard S. Childs.[1] Here, the meaning of the text is not accessed by means of a literary analysis but by asking how the text contributes to, and is in turn constrained by, the larger canon of Scripture of which it forms a part. What is needed is close attention to the Bible as it stands, rather than an excavation of the text as if it were merely another ancient document of purely historical interest to us. Childs argued that if we begin, as historical critics

---

[1] See Brevard S. Childs, *Introduction to the Old Testament as Scripture* (Philadelphia: Fortress, 1979); idem, *Biblical Theology of the Old and New Testaments: Theological Reflection on the Christian Bible* (London: SCM, 1992).

traditionally do, by ignoring the Bible's religious claim on us, and studying it as though it were a document that has just happened to turn up from the ancient world, we will be bound to have difficulty in subsequently making connections with our own belief. But that problem would be of our own making: if one takes Christianity's sacred text and insists on ignoring its sacredness, then one is bound to find it hard to move from the mode of study one has chosen back into a theological appropriation. What the Christian who studies the Bible should do, on the contrary, is to *begin* by treating the Bible as the Church's book. That will not preclude asking "historical" questions about it – indeed Childs's canonical interpretation is heavily, if not entirely, dependent on the historical-critical results available in his day – but such questions will be clearly seen as secondary to the task of expounding the text as it now is, in the form in which Christians and Jews have canonized it.

There can be no doubt that this represents a new position in modern biblical studies. As I have tried to argue elsewhere, it was anticipated in some measure by earlier biblical scholars.[2] Gerhard von Rad, for example, already sought an appreciation of the whole text, beyond the fragmentation brought about by source criticism, and there is a general movement of thought going back to Karl Barth (a clear influence on von Rad) that insists on reading the Bible as the Word of God, and not merely as an ancient document. The "Biblical Theology" movement, as Childs himself stresses, had the same vision of biblical study as part of the Church's theological task, rather than as an "antiquarian" pursuit.[3] But in the form

---

[2] See John Barton, "Canon and Old Testament Interpretation," in *In Search of True Wisdom: Essays in Old Testament Interpretation in Honour of Ronald E. Clements* (ed. E. Ball; JSOTSup 300; Sheffield: Sheffield Academic Press, 1999), 37–52.

[3] See Brevard S. Childs, *Biblical Theology in Crisis* (Philadelphia: Fortress, 1970).

it now takes, Childs's program is certainly a new departure. His whole approach has stimulated many who do not subscribe to it in full to nevertheless ask questions about the Bible "as Scripture" in a new way, and it is now normal to read papers and books concentrating on the "final form" of the biblical text and treating the Bible as a whole in a way that would have been distinctly unusual thirty years ago in academic study of the Bible. The whole ethos of current biblical studies, especially in North America, owes much to these new questions that Childs has placed on the agenda.

The second and third approaches to the interpretation of whole books in their final form have many superficial resemblances. In both cases, we are urged to look at what lies before us on the page, not at what may (or may not) have preceded it in the text's long history of composition and transmission. But appearances can deceive. When Childs talks of the "final form" of the text he does not mean the text as a unified aesthetic object, but (Barth-like) as the communication of the word of God. This communication may be aided by recognizing features of the history of the text: for example, the Deutero-Isaiah hypothesis is illuminating for faith because it enables us to see that words once directed to a specific set of circumstances have been incorporated into a larger work (the book of Isaiah) and so set free to speak to all generations. The question is not: "What does the final form mean as a literary unity?" but rather, "What word of God is communicated through this passage?" Since church and synagogue have canonized a particular form of the text, it must be through that form that theological insight is meant to be generated. It may well be illuminated in some ways by our knowing about the background of the text – historical, archaeological, text-critical, even source-critical. But the essential point to hold on to is what our exegesis should be directed toward: knowledge of God through Scripture.

That aim can never be attained if we ignore the form in which the Bible has come down to us, as though the Church had canonized "J" or "First Isaiah." Knowledge of the process that led up to canonization can certainly be illuminating, but only as long as it is recognized as *ancillary* to the theological task.

As will be clear from what I have written elsewhere about the canonical approach, I do not subscribe to it as a program.[4] But "canonical criticism" as it is sometimes called (though Childs disliked the term because it sounded as if it were just one more "criticism" in the biblical scholar's toolbox, rather than a distinct and comprehensive approach) can be practiced even by those who do not think of it as the ideal or exclusive model for biblical interpretation. Hence, we can, with perfect reason, ask what a canonical critic would be likely to say about a text such as the finished book of Amos.

We will now look in more detail at the three approaches just outlined.

REDACTION AND COMPOSITION CRITICISM

Most biblical scholars believe that when later editors or scribes added short passages to the prophetic books, they intended these passages to modify, cumulatively, the meaning of the whole book; they were not simply to be read as the insertions that they actually were. It is possible to argue, on the contrary, that the effect was to make the prophetic book in question into an anthology, with no overall theme or meaning. In this section, however, we will proceed on the assumption that the oracles we have identified

---

[4] See, e.g., John Barton, *Reading the Old Testament: Method in Biblical Study* (2nd ed.; London: Darton, Longman & Todd, 1996), 89–103.

as additions to Amos were not meant to be read simply on their own as isolated fragments, but were intended to shape the reader's perception of the meaning of the entire book.

This is probably most obvious in the case of the epilogue, where the presence at the very end of the book of a prophecy predicting the restoration of Judah and a new Davidic empire slants the entire book in a quite different direction from what most scholars think was the original intention of Amos, with his predictions of unalterable doom. It is possible that the epilogue originally had an independent existence before it was attached to the book of Amos, as part of a large floating collection of oracles of blessing that were circulating in the time of the exile or soon after it. We should then owe its presence in the book as it now stands to a redactor who picked it up and added it to the end of the book as it existed in his day. But it is equally possible that it was specifically composed for its present position as a radical reinterpretation of the message of Amos – a piece of *Fortschreibung* that changed the thrust of the book in a new direction. In any case, whoever placed it where it now is, whether that person wrote it from scratch or borrowed it from elsewhere, surely meant it to change the import of the whole book. In this, it is not unlike the endings to Hosea or Qoheleth, which also add interpretative glosses to the whole book in ways that do not necessarily conform to the book's original intent:

> Those who are wise understand these things;
>> those who are discerning know them.
> For the ways of the LORD are right,
>> and the upright walk in them,
>> but transgressors stumble in them. (Hos 14:9)

> The end of the matter; all has been heard. Fear God, and keep his commandments; for that is the whole duty of everyone. For God will bring every deed into judgment, including every secret thing, whether good or evil. (Eccl 12:13–14)

The ending to Hosea has the effect of turning the time-bound prophetic sayings into a collection of wisdom aphorisms, true at all times; while the last verses of Qoheleth nullify the author's scepticism about divine judgment by asserting that God really does judge humankind after all. In effect, the meaning of the whole book of Ecclesiastes is reversed by the addition of these two verses, which can hardly be an originally independent fragment that has just happened to be attached here. Instead, the verses are a quite deliberate example of *Fortschreibung*.

A redaction-critical or composition-critical approach thus tends to see the latest additions to the book as determining how it is meant to be read, for that is why these sections were added. One obviously redactional addition to Amos is the superscription (1:1), which identifies the whole book as the words of the prophet from Tekoa and makes it like many of the other prophetic books:

> The words of Amos, who was among the shepherds of Tekoa, which he saw concerning Israel in the days of King Uzziah of Judah and in the days of King Jeroboam son of Joash of Israel, two years before the earthquake.

This underscores the point made in the (equally secondary) oracle at 3:7, that YHWH reveals his intentions to a succession of prophetic figures. This may falsify the true message of Amos himself, who (like Jeremiah later) was concerned to distance himself from the teachings of "prophets" and to establish himself as uniquely inspired by YHWH rather than belonging to a professional class of prophets:

> Then Amos answered Amaziah, "I am no prophet, nor a prophet's son; but I am a herdsman, and a dresser of sycamore trees, and the LORD took me from following the flock, and the LORD said to me, 'Go, prophesy to my people Israel.'" (Amos 7:14–15)
>
> I have heard what the prophets have said who prophesy lies in my name, saying, "I have dreamed, I have dreamed!" How long? Will

the hearts of the prophets ever turn back – those who prophesy lies, and who prophesy the deceit of their own heart? They plan to make my people forget my name by their dreams that they tell one another, just as their ancestors forgot my name for Baal. Let the prophet who has a dream tell the dream, but let the one who has my word speak my word faithfully. What has straw in common with wheat? says the LORD. Is not my word like fire, says the LORD, and like a hammer that breaks rock in pieces? See, therefore, I am against the prophets, says the LORD, who steal my words from one another. See, I am against the prophets, says the LORD, who use their own tongues and say, "Says the LORD." (Jer 23:25–31)

But as it now stands, the superscription does make Amos seem like the other prophets. It also, of course, dates him and tells us about his secular occupation. The superscription may belong to the very last level of redaction, when the book was being fitted for its place in the "Book of the Twelve."

In Amos 1:2, we have an oracle also found in Joel 3:16 (Heb 4:16), which gives Amos's message a Judah-centered slant: the God who is to pass judgment on the northern kingdom is the God whose actual home is in Zion:

> The LORD roars from Zion,
>   And utters his voice from Jerusalem;
> The pastures of the shepherds wither,
>   And the top of Carmel dries up. (Amos 1:2)

One does not get the impression from the words of Amos that he espoused this idea himself: YHWH for him is a God naturally at home in northern Israel, and indeed the freedom and independence of YHWH makes it doubtful whether Amos really saw him as "residing" anywhere on earth. Amos seems to have held to quite an advanced monotheism in which God was not locatable in one place. But subsequent generations in Israel and Judah reverted to the more commonplace ancient idea that the god had a dwelling place, even if the earthly abode was not his only one but in some way mirrored a heavenly throne.[5] For the redactor, the book of Amos was to be read as the utterances of the God of Jerusalem through Amos. This God judged the northern kingdom primarily, but probably Judah as well, since by this stage there already existed the Judah oracle (2:4–5) and the reference to Zion as parallel to Samaria in 6:1. Judah was the true home of Yhwh, and the northern kingdom was in some measure foreign. This makes sense in the postexilic age when there was no longer a northern kingdom, and when the current inhabitants of what had been its territory, centered in Samaria, were regarded as half-Jews at best. By this time, God was seen as the God of the Judeans primarily, though (as Amos himself had believed) his reach extends to other areas, including what had been the northern kingdom.

The idea of Yhwh roaring like a lion may draw on the oracle in chapter 3:

> The lion has roared;
>> who will not fear?
> The Lord God has spoken;
>> who can but prophesy? (Amos 3:8)

But lion imagery for God is found in other prophets too:

> As a lion or a young lion growls over its prey,
>> and – when a band of shepherds is called out against it –
> is not terrified by their shouting
>> or daunted at their noise,
> so the Lord of hosts will come down
>> to fight upon Mount Zion and upon its hill. (Isa 31:4)

> So I will become like a lion to them,
>> like a leopard I will lurk beside the way.

---

5 Cf. Psalms 11:4: "The Lord is in his holy temple, the Lord's throne is in heaven."

> I will fall upon them like a bear robbed of her cubs,
>   and will tear open the covering of their heart;
> there I will devour them like a lion,
>   as a wild animal would mangle them. (Hos 13:7–8)

So, the addition of Amos 1:2 correctly perceives his message to have been primarily one of doom, causing natural disaster: the lion's roar is like a blight in its effect ("the pastures of the shepherds wither").[6]

The overall effect of most of the additions, however, is not to undergird Amos's message of disaster, but to qualify it. Doom is not the book's last word, but instead it ends on a note of hope and blessing in the epilogue. The message of the finished book is that Yhwh has purposes for Israel that are ultimately good and beneficial. Punishment is severe, but it is only one episode in the longer history of Yhwh's dealings with Israel: he rescued Israel from Egypt in the beginning (3:1: "the whole family that I brought up out of the land of Egypt"), and despite their disobedience has remained and will remain their God. He will certainly punish them for their sins – and, for the redactors of the book, this punishment had already happened, in the form of the exile – but beyond punishment, he will bring them back to prosperity under a new Davidic monarchy.[7] Not only will the nation be restored to the legendary prosperity it had enjoyed in the time of David, but even the natural world will be transformed to provide miraculous

---

[6] For an extended study of the lion image, including its negative valences in Amos, see Brent A. Strawn, *What Is Stronger than a Lion? Leonine Image and Metaphor in the Hebrew Bible and the Ancient Near East* (OBO 212; Fribourg: Academic Press, 2005), esp. 58–65.

[7] This message is very similar to that in the final version of the book of Hosea. In the case of that book, too, we may speculate that the prophet's original message was harsh and unforgiving, but, as it now stands, the book promises salvation beyond judgment.

fruitfulness (9:13), and Israel will be guaranteed a dwelling place in its land for all time to come (9:14–15). Thus the book has a hopeful message, vastly at odds with what Amos himself probably taught.

Indeed, the final form of the book presents something like a worked-out theology, far removed from the "occasional" character of Amos's own words. Like all the prophets, Amos reacted to particular situations and gave what he believed to be the word of YHWH that bore on the immediate concerns of the people around him. Later redactors saw the prophetic books as relevant for all time, and so adapted them to produce a conscious theological scheme. For the redactor, YHWH, though he had clear authority over the whole world, was first and foremost the God of Israel (meaning in practice in his day the God of Yehud, the small Persian-controlled state that occupied some of what had been Judah). YHWH lived in the Temple in Jerusalem – not quite literally or exclusively, for he had a throne in heaven, but still he was associated with that place above all others, and it was from there that he uttered oracles through prophets. These prophets formed a line of succession, probably thought of as going back to Moses (as taught in Deuteronomy), and their function was to warn the people of the consequences of sin, but also, and above all, to set out YHWH's long-term plan.[8] The theology of the redactors contained a distinctive eschatology, in the sense of a divine plan for all time, in which, after many vicissitudes, the people of YHWH would be settled permanently in the Holy Land, never again to be removed from it by any enemies. They would be ruled over by a restored Davidic line. YHWH as a cosmic God, celebrated in the "doxologies" as having the power

---

[8] See my comments in John Barton, *Oracles of God: Perceptions of Ancient Prophecy in Israel after the Exile* (2nd ed.; New York: Oxford University Press, 2007 [1st ed.: 1986]), 214–234.

both to create and to destroy, was fully capable of bringing about this long-term consummation of his plans for Israel, and because he ruled over the natural as well as the political world, he could also guarantee that there would be an abundance of produce for the people to live on into the indefinite future. There is no hint of an otherworldly eschatology in the book of Amos, but then that hardly exists in the Old Testament at all.[9]

If we want to see how the finished theology of the book of Amos fitted into the theological assumptions of the Persian age, we have only to look at Zechariah, where there are the same themes of renewed political life, fruitfulness in crop yields, and peaceful life in the Promised Land:

> But now I will not deal with the remnant of this people as in the former days, says the LORD of hosts. For there shall be a sowing of peace; the vine shall yield its fruit, the ground shall give its produce, and the skies shall give their dew; and I will cause the remnant of this people to possess all these things. Just as you have been a cursing among the nations, O house of Judah and house of Israel, so I will save you and you shall be a blessing. Do not be afraid, but let your hands be strong. (Zech 8:11–13)

The finished book of Amos fits perfectly into this world of thought. All the doom and destruction was indeed foretold by YHWH through his prophet, but it is now over: the people have the times of suffering behind them, and from now on can expect only blessing from the hand of YHWH, just as Zechariah had foretold:

> The word of the LORD of hosts came to me, saying: Thus says the LORD of hosts: The fast of the fourth month, and the fast of the fifth, and the fast of the seventh, and the fast of the tenth, shall be

---

[9]   A classic study, arguing that otherworldly eschatology arose in the late postexilic period, is Sigmund Mowinckel, *He That Cometh* (trans. G. W. Anderson; Oxford: Basil Blackwell, 1956), see esp. 261–279.

> seasons of joy and gladness, and cheerful festivals for the house of Judah: therefore love truth and peace. (Zech 8:18–19)

Thus the redaction of the book of Amos could be seen as implying that most of the oracles in the book, which were so urgent and devastating in the mouth of Amos and in the ears of his contemporaries, belonged in a past period of time, when Yhwh had destructive intentions toward Israel *but which he has now accomplished and exhausted*. The book tells a story of past history, and its relevance to the present does not lie in any revival of the harsh message of the prophet but in its presentation of the terrible suffering that culminated in the exile – though that is now over and done with. Amos said that Israel would be exiled "beyond Damascus" (5:27), and the prophetic word, which always comes true, had not failed: Israel had indeed been exiled, to Babylonia. But he had also had a message for a time after this terrible event, a message of renewed divine approval and blessing, and this, not the prediction of destruction, was his final word:

> I will plant them upon their land,
> and they shall never again be plucked up
> out of the land that I have given them,
> says the Lord your God. (Amos 9:15)

The final form of Amos is thus a coherent book setting out a coherent theology. That theology is unlikely to be the original theology of the prophet Amos. It makes sense, rather, against the backdrop of the reconstruction of life in Yehud after there had been a partial return from exile and old hopes for the monarchy were stirring again – possibly attaching themselves to the person of Zerubbabel, the Persian-appointed governor who was evidently of the Judean royal line (cf. Hag 1:1; 2:13; Zech 4:8–10). From a redaction-critical or compositional-critical point of view, therefore, the book of

Amos is a "normal" postexilic prophetic book teaching about the power of YHWH, his providence in the governance of the world and especially in the choice of Israel, and his guidance of the nation through apostasy and punishment into a new age of blessing and serenity. No longer would the people err by worshipping "foreign" gods as they had done in the past, but instead they would be loyal to YHWH, since apostates would have been removed from the community for good. Israel would again be God's faithful people, and he in turn would keep them safe.

LITERARY CRITICISM

Redaction- or compositional-critical approaches to a text depend on prior source-critical analysis. Only when we have identified the original core and the additions can we see how the meaning of the core has been altered by adding later materials, and only then can we attempt to describe the overall meaning that the book has acquired through its redaction. It is possible, however, to read the book in its finished form without paying any attention to the history of its composition, a good bit of which is speculative anyway. This is the approach that has come to be known as a "literary" or synchronic reading in the last few decades.[10] Some forms of it do not differ greatly in their results from redaction/composition criticism, even though the underlying theoretical basis is different,

[10] A leading exponent is Robert Alter. See his *The Art of Biblical Narrative* (New York: Basic Books, 1981); idem, *The Art of Biblical Poetry* (Edinburgh: T & T Clark, 1990); idem, *The World of Biblical Literature* (New York: Basic Books, 1992); idem, *The David Story: A Translation with Commentary of 1 & 2 Samuel* (New York and London: W. W. Norton, 1999); idem, *The Five Books of Moses: A Translation with Commentary* (New York and London: W. W. Norton, 2004); and idem, *The Book of Psalms* (New York and London: W. W. Norton, 2007). See also Robert Alter and Frank Kermode, eds., *The Literary Guide to the Bible* (Cambridge: Belknap Press of Harvard University, 1987).

since, as we have seen, redactional additions tend to have the effect of conditioning how we read the rest or the entirety of the book – often being located in strategic places, such as the beginning and end of the work in question. In the case of Amos, a literary reading, like a redaction-critical one, might well concentrate on the ending and see it as a dénouement, giving us the answer to the question of how the book as a whole is to be construed. Overall, Amos's book moves from darkness to light, and a literary reading might well see that as the main "message" it conveys: disaster followed by blessing, the theme of much Jewish and Christian theology. It is rather like the book of Judges, where apostasy and punishment is regularly followed by repentance and restoration, except that this is not presented as a cyclical scheme (as arguably it is in Judges) but as the shape of world history as a whole. The story of Israel as the book of Amos presents it is, we could say, a comedy rather than a tragedy.

The term "comedy" is in fact used in an important study of the finished form of the prophetic books by Paul House.[11] He sees the whole Book of the Twelve as moving through disaster to blessing, with Amos, so near the beginning of the collection, predominantly dark but still already containing some hope at its end – a kind of example in miniature of the shape of the whole of the Twelve. A similar emphasis can be found in the work of James Nogalski.[12] R. E. Clements has argued that all the prophetic books have a

---

[11] Paul R. House, *The Unity of the Twelve* (JSOTSup 97; Sheffield: Sheffield Academic Press, 1990). Ehud Ben Zvi has sharply criticized the idea that the Book of the Twelve is to be seen as a unity, arguing that it is simply an anthology of twelve separate books. See his "Twelve Prophetic Books or 'The Twelve'? A Few Preliminary Considerations," in *Forming Prophetic Literature: Essays on Isaiah and the Twelve in Honor of John D. W. Watts* (eds. J. W. Watts and P. R. House; JSOTSup 235; Sheffield: Sheffield Academic Press, 1996), 125–156.

[12] See James Nogalski, *Literary Precursors to the Book of the Twelve* (BZAW 217; Berlin: Walter de Gruyter, 1993).

similar shape, moving from bad to good, and indeed this is often true in miniature of smaller sections within them: the book of Isaiah, for example, has alternating blocks of judgment oracles and oracles of blessing and restoration.[13] It seems clear that, in Second Temple Judaism, it became normal to see the prophetic message as having this twofold character, and nearly all the prophetic books as they now stand exhibit such a pattern. The prophets as a whole, and each one individually, therefore, stand as witnesses that "he strikes, but his hands heal" (Job 5:18). This is also, arguably, the shape of the Deuteronomistic History, which traces the descent of Israel into destruction and darkness but ends on a small rising note with the release of Jehoiachin from prison (2 Kgs 25:27–30); and even more so the shape of the books of Chronicles, which end with the permission given by Cyrus for Jews to return to Jerusalem (2 Chr 36:22–23, cf. Ezra 1:2–4). In brief, Old Testament books often have a "happy ending." But this is far from facile: the road to restoration, especially as we see it in Amos, lies through terrible and unspeakable suffering for the nation (cf., e.g., in Amos, 5:3 with 6:9). But in the end – at the very end – light triumphs over darkness.

I have said that a literary reading, like a redaction/compositional-critical one, is likely to fixate on the end of the book as giving a clue to its meaning because that is how people in the modern West habitually read books. It is worth noting, however, that it may not have been the characteristic way of reading in the ancient world, so that a historically informed literary criticism might conceivably take a different route. In the first chapter of this study, I introduced

---

[13] R. E. Clements, "Patterns in the Prophetic Canon," in idem, *Old Testament Prophecy: From Oracles to Canon* (Louisville: Westminster John Knox, 1996), 191–202.

the theory that the arrangement of the book of Amos, or of significant parts of it, might be chiastic or concentric in shape. Back in
1977, J. de Waard argued that 5:1–17, a very early part of the book, is
chiastic in structure.[14] N. J. Tromp proposed that the whole of 4:1–
6:7 forms an extended chiasmus,[15] while R. Bryan Widbin thinks
that chapters 3–6 are chiastic.[16] Since this scholarly discussion has
progressed from a smaller to a larger passage, but all with the same
core, the three hypotheses are mutually compatible. As we have
seen, there may also be a chiastic structure in the complementar-
ity of the five visions in chapters 7–9 (minus some additions) and
the original five oracles against the nations in chapters 1–2. Now,
one of the effects of chiasm is to transfer attention from the beginning and end of a book to the center, the point where the structure
"turns."[17] A chiastic hypothesis for the book might thus highlight
not 1:1–2 or 9:13–15 but 5:7–10:

> Seek the LORD and live,
>> or he will break out against the house of Joseph like fire,
>> and it will devour Bethel, with no one to quench it.

[14] J. de Waard, "The Chiastic Structure of Amos V,1–17," *VT* 27 (1977): 170–177.
[15] N. J. Tromp, "Amos V 1–17: Towards a Stylistic and Rhetorical Analysis," in
*Prophets, Worship and Theodicy: Studies in Prophetism, Biblical Theology
and Structural and Rhetorical Analysis and on the Place of Music in Worship:
Papers Read at the Joint British–Dutch Old Testament Conference held at
Woudschoten, 1982* (OtSt 23; Leiden: Brill, 1984), 65–85.
[16] R. Bryan Widbin, "Center Structure in the Center Oracles of Amos," in *"Go to
the Land I Will Show You": Studies in Honor of Dwight W. Young* (eds. J. E.
Coleson and V. H. Matthews; Winona Lake: Eisenbrauns, 1996), 177–192.
[17] See Nathan Klaus, *Pivot Patterns in the Former Prophets* (JSOTSup 247;
Sheffield: Sheffield Academic Press, 1999); and Jerome T. Walsh, *Style and
Structure in Biblical Hebrew Narrative* (Collegeville, MN: Liturgical, 2001).
John W. Welch, ed., *Chiasmus in Antiquity* (Hildesheim: Gerstenberger
Verlag, 1981) contains a number of studies on the phenomenon in ancient
texts. Note especially Yehuda Radday's contribution, "Chiasmus in Hebrew
Biblical Narrative" (50–117).

Ah, you that turn justice to wormwood,
  and bring righteousness to the ground!

The one who made the Pleiades and Orion,
  and turns deep darkness into the morning,
  and darkens the day into night,
who calls for the waters of the sea,
  and pours them out upon the surface of the earth,
the LORD is his name,
who makes destruction flash out against the strong,
  so that destruction comes upon the fortress.

They hate the one who reproves in the gate,
  and they abhor the one who speaks the truth.

Verses 7 and 10 consist of Amos's characteristic attack on social injustice, and the central section, vv. 8–9, are the "doxology" in which God darkens the morning into deep night. If we take this central point of the book as the clue to its overall message, then we seem to be back with something like the original message of the prophet Amos (even though the doxology is probably "inauthentic" – but that does not matter for a literary reading). The book, read chiastically, may open with God resident in Jerusalem and end with marvellous fruitfulness, but at its very center – the worm in the bud, as it were – lies a dark message about God the destroyer. This subverts the apparently "positive" message that emerges from the book if we read it in a typically linear, "Western" way, with attention to the "happy ending," and throws us back on a far bleaker theme. God may promise blessings on Israel, but are they unconditional? Perhaps the book is constructed to warn us that Amos's message of judgment on social sins remains in force, even in the near-paradisal conditions of the renewed land and nation. The warning of coming destruction is not abrogated, then, but is new in each generation that confronts YHWH, who at any time can "darken the day into night." Earthquakes happen again and again, and there is no guaranteed security from them, nor from the other kinds of divine judgment of which they serve as the archetype.

This reading may seem artificial, dependent on a literary analysis of the book that is far from obvious and only emerges through detailed attention to the text. But ancient books were often cleverly constructed, and there are other chiastic or concentric passages in the Old Testament, for example, Isaiah 6:10 (note the reversal of "eyes" and "ears") and Jonah 1:1–16, where Jonah's confession in v. 9 forms the pivot of the passage.[18] The book of Lamentations probably exhibits such a structure, and there the effect is the opposite of that in Amos, since the center of the book is the one place where hope for restoration appears:

> But this I call to mind,
>   and therefore I have hope.
> The steadfast love of the LORD never ceases,
>   his mercies never come to an end;
> they are new every morning;
>   great is your faithfulness.
> "The LORD is my portion," says my soul,
>   "therefore I will hope in him."
> The LORD is good to those who wait for him,
>   to the soul that seeks him.
> It is good that one should wait quietly
>   for the salvation of the LORD.
> It is good for one to bear
>   the yoke in youth,
> to sit alone in silence,
>   when the LORD has imposed it,
> to put one's mouth to the dust
>   (there may yet be hope),
> to give one's cheek to the smiter,
>   and be filled with insults.

---

[18] See further the literature cited in the previous note.

> For the LORD will not
> > reject for ever.
> Although he causes grief, he will have compassion
> > according to the abundance of his steadfast love;
> for he does not willingly afflict
> > or grieve anyone. (Lam 3:21–33)

This is the central passage of the chapter, and also the central passage of the book, and it may be argued that by presenting hope in this crucial place the compiler is inviting the reader to see hope as the ultimate message.[19]

Similarly, there is no reason why we should not read Amos in the light of the chiastic arrangement, and if we do, then its theology is much darker than the scheme outlined in the section on redaction criticism above. It is precisely because the book in general presents such a gloomy aspect that the hypothesis that the epilogue is a later addition has struck so many people as plausible. Amos is thought of, where he is thought of at all, as a prophet of doom. A literary reading does not in itself commit us to ignoring this common perception, but is free to regard the epilogue as a kind of afterthought, or even as a prediction of a coming state of blessing in which, however, the possibility of repeating the mistakes of the past and consequently reaping the same dire consequences is not ruled out.[20] Whatever may have been the case in the days of Haggai and Zechariah, later Judaism had strands that still

---

[19] See Norman K. Gottwald, "Lamentations," in *Harper's Bible Commentary* (ed. James L. Mays; San Francisco: Harper & Row, 1988), 647: "the strongest statement of faith and hope, underscored by the triple acrostic and even by repetition of the same acrostic word (note the threefold 'good' as the acrostic term in 3:25–27), is positioned at the center of the work." Cf. also Jill Middlemas, "The Violent Storm in Lamentations," *JSOT* 29 (2004): 81–97.

[20] A point Childs makes as well. See his *Introduction*, 407 (cited fully in the next section).

foretold judgment on the nation, or at least on the wicked within it, if it sinned. Rabbinic eschatology believed in the coming judgment of Israel as well as of the Gentiles, and Christianity did not think that even the salvation brought in Christ, which was supposed to exceed all previous expectations, ruled out the possibility of national or corporate judgment if God was provoked into anger by sin (see Heb 3:12–4:13; Jude 5–16). Thus there is a possible literary reading that does not treat the epilogue as annulling the uncompromising message of judgment that so permeates most of the book, but regards the book as an awful warning despite its occasional promises of hope and restoration.

It is hard to know how one could adjudicate between these different kinds of literary readings. Modern Western literature tends to see the end of a work as particularly important in arriving at the meaning of the whole; in some ancient cultures, however, it may have been the center of a work that dominated. So, a reading focused on the center, and alert for signals such as chiasmus or concentrism, might seem to be preferable from an historical point of view. But a modern literary reading may not feel constrained by the text's original intention. One might argue that whatever the compiler of Amos meant by the way the book is arranged, we are free to read it with modern conventions if we are interpreting it in a modern context. Once the likely "original sense" of the text is abandoned as a criterion for our reading of it, it is perfectly possible to interpret it as though it were a modern work and operated with modern conventions. The issue here is a much-discussed one, which takes us far beyond the detail of the book of Amos proper and into general literary theory writ large.[21]

---

[21]   See further my *Reading the Old Testament*, 180–219.

CANONICAL READINGS

There is a third route to a holistic reading of the book of Amos, and that is to see it as part of the canon of Scripture and to ask what it contributes if seen in that wider context. Here, the meaning of Amos depends not on features immanent to this book alone, but also to its position in the Book of the Twelve, in the prophetic corpus, in the Old Testament, perhaps even in the whole (Christian) Bible. If we follow the approach first set out by Childs, we might arrive at a "canonical meaning" of Amos. What might this look like? Probably, with Rolf Rendtorff, we will end up saying that the book tells us that "the day of the Lord is both darkness and light."[22] In other words, we will not need to prioritize one part of the book above another – neither the ending over the core, nor the core over the ending. Instead, we will adopt a pluralistic approach, believing that there is theological truth in both the declaration of coming judgment and in the promises of salvation. The book of Amos speaks of both, exemplifying the truth that Martin Luther saw as central to the Old Testament, that "The LORD kills and brings to life; he brings down to Sheol and raises up" (1 Sam 2:6). It may be argued that, in the religion to which the Old Testament (or even the whole Christian Bible?) bears witness, there is room for both hope

---

[22] Rolf Rendtorff, "How to Read the Book of the Twelve as a Theological Unity," in Society of Biblical Literature 1997 Seminar Papers (Altanta: Society of Biblical Literature, 1997), 420–432, reprinted in Reading and Hearing the Book of the Twelve (eds. M. Sweeney and J. Nogalski; SBLSymS 36; Atlanta: Society of Biblical Literature, 2000), 75–87, and also in Rolf Rendtorff, Der Text in seiner Endgestalt: Schritte auf dem Weg zu einer Theologie des Alten Testaments (Neukirchen-Vluyn: Neukirchener Verlag, 2001), 139–151. See also idem, "Alas for the Day! The 'Day of the Lord' in the Book of the Twelve," in God in the Fray: A Tribute to Walter Brueggemann (eds. T. Linafelt and T. K. Beal; Minneapolis: Fortress, 1998), 186–197, reprinted in Rolf Rendtorff, Der Text in seiner Endgestalt, 253–264.

and fear – the overall theology of the Bible expresses confidence in God's beneficent purposes so long as his will is obeyed, and the book of Amos in its finished form bears witness to that idea.

Childs himself in his *Introduction to the Old Testament as Scripture* comments on the "canonical shape" of the book of Amos, and, like Rendtorff, argues that the hopeful message of the epilogue does not annul the message of doom (as it arguably does in the redaction/composition-critical model), but combines with it to produce a nuanced argument in which both doom and hope are conjoined:

> [T]he restriction which is introduced in [chapter 9 v.]8b assumes the complete destruction of the kingdom of Israel (9–10). It does not weaken or undercut the severity or extent of the judgment. No segment of Israel escapes the judgment, as Amos had truly prophesied. The restriction has to do with the ultimate purpose of God in the future of Israel. The discourse moves into the realm of eschatology (11, 13). It turns on the possibility of a new existence after the end has come. The promise concerns the raising up of the shattered "booth of David" – that is, David's larger kingdom, which can again lay claim on the land. No human ruler can achieve this feat; the initiative lies solely with God. The hope is miraculous and logically incomprehensible. It is placed within the eschatological framework of the latter days. That the continuity which the new shares with the old has been established from God's side is indicated by the mythopoetic language of the return of paradise.
>
> The redaction of chapter 9 does not soften Amos's message of total judgment against sinful Israel by allowing a pious remnant to escape. The destruction is fully confirmed (vv. 9b, 11). Rather, the editor effects a decisive canonical shaping of the book by placing Amos's words within a broader eschatological framework which transcends the perspective of the prophet himself. Only from the divine perspective is there a hope beyond the destruction seen by Amos.[23]

---

[23] Childs, *Introduction*, 407.

Childs's reading of the canonical meaning of the book thus says something about the freedom and omnipotence of God, and shows that God takes the initiative in planning a future for Israel beyond judgment. Less depends on obedient human response for Childs than for Rendtorff, and there is a greater stress on God as the sole cause of Israel's salvation.

A "canonical" perspective might do justice to one set of (what historical critics regard as) additions, namely the "doxologies." Though what we most notice about these texts is probably their negative tone, they in fact speak of Yhwh as the source of both darkness and light. Amos 5:8–9 says that Yhwh "turns deep darkness into the morning," not only that he "darkens the day into night." There is resemblance here to Isaiah 45:7:

> I form light and create darkness,
>> I make weal and create woe.
>> I the Lord do all these things.

Amos, then, is not a smooth text that neutralizes disaster through a message of eventual restoration *or* a text that neutralizes blessing through a message of doom, but a witness to the paradoxical character of God's way of acting in the world. The "doxologies" are not the praises of a purely benign God, but also express his dark side. And yet, to put it the other way around, they are also not purely laments about the destruction God can bring, but praise of God as the one who orders the cosmos. A canonical reading of Amos might well try to do justice to this ambiguity.

Why, after all, does the Old Testament contain prophetic texts? Historical criticism does not really ask this question: the prophets are ancient texts that were part of the library of ancient Israel, and so have been preserved, with all sorts of redactional additions, down to our own day. A "canonical" critic, however, is likely to want to know what theological freight the books have, and may well see them as part of the witness in Judaism (and Christianity) to the involvement of God in human affairs. That involvement is not a simple matter of directing the course of either a nation's or an individual's life, but is a story of the interplay between divine will and human freedom. Theological reflection on this interplay will see the events that happen on earth as bearing witness to both human and divine intentions and actions. And the Hebrew prophets were the first, and perhaps the greatest, to perform this kind of reflection within the life of ancient Israel. The texts they left, however much these are the result of subsequent redaction, bear witness to the whole complex process by which God's wishes, intentions, and actions, and those of his human partners, intermingle: sometimes bringing joy and sometimes suffering. The very ambiguity of a book such as Amos is thus fruitful because it allows all sides of this complex interrelationship to emerge without foreclosing any options.

A THEOLOGY OF AMOS?

Is there a theology of the book of Amos? The argument in this chapter has been that there are several possible theologies of the book, depending on our theoretical model for establishing the "message" that a biblical book conveys. Redaction/composition criticism on the whole locates the overall meaning in the changes made by the latest contributors to the book, since these contributors are seen as shaping the book through additions, precisely in order to convey their own message. Literary readings will look to the shape and structure of the work without raising questions about which sections are "original" and which are later additions, and, as we have seen, this may lead to strikingly different accounts of the book's overall theology, since this approach is at liberty to foreground elements that are not later additions to a core but may be part of that core itself. The "shape" of a biblical book may not be linear but may be, for example, concentric, and, in that case, the kernel of its meaning may lie in the center, not at the beginning or at the end. Finally, attention to the book's place and role in the overall canon may suggest other kinds of meaning that it may convey, as one voice among a chorus rather than as a single speaker with a message all its own. The meaning conveyed by the whole canon of Scripture may be seen as highly plural, or it may be seen as essentially unified – most scholars who adopt the canonical approach tend in the unitary direction – and a book such as Amos contributes only one strand to the overall tapestry, whether or not this tapestry forms a harmonious whole.

CHAPTER 6

The Reception of the Theology of Amos

So far, we have looked at what modern scholarship can tell us of the original teaching of Amos against its contemporary background, and of the meaning the book acquired through its various stages of redaction and incorporation into the collection that is the Old Testament. But how did past readers receive and understand what the book was saying?

AMOS IN ANCIENT ISRAEL, IN THE EARLY CHURCH, AND AT QUMRAN

In one sense, Amos was a very important theological influence on those who came after him. Even in the eighth century, there is good reason to think that Isaiah was familiar with his words, as was argued by Reinhard Fey back in 1963.[1] A message of uncompromising doom becomes normative for biblical prophecy, as we read in the story of Jeremiah's confrontation with Hananiah:

> Then the prophet Jeremiah spoke to the prophet Hananiah in the presence of the priests and all the people who were standing in the house of the LORD; and the prophet Jeremiah said, "Amen! May

---

[1] Reinhard Fey, *Amos und Jesaja: Abhängigkeit und Eigenständigkeit des Jesaja* (WMANT 12; Neukirchen-Vluyn: Neukirchener Verlag, 1963).

the LORD do so; may the LORD fulfill the words that you have prophesied, and bring back to this place from Babylon the vessels of the house of the LORD, and all the exiles. But listen now to this word that I speak in your hearing and in the hearing of all the people. The prophets who preceded you and me from ancient times prophesied war, famine, and pestilence against many countries and great kingdoms. As for the prophet who prophesies peace, when the word of that prophet comes true, then it will be known that the LORD has truly sent the prophet." (Jer 28:5–9)

This image of the prophet as a purveyor of a message of imminent disaster surely depends on Amos: we know that prophets in the ancient Near East in general did *not* prophesy in these terms, and the prevalence of judgment prophecy in ancient Israel from the eighth century onwards almost certainly derives from the fact that Amos had set the trend. Yet there are no overt references to his words. We might remember that in general the prophets hardly ever cite each other, and Amos and Hosea, who were certainly very near contemporaries, both of whom worked in the North, do not have any reciprocal references. Prophets in Israel in general do not seem to have appealed to past "authorities," but apparently spoke freely as they felt moved by YHWH.[2] In the same way, as we have seen, even though Amos probably refers to existing written laws, he never says that he is doing so, but speaks as though on his own authority – "not as the scribes." But he established the mode in which subsequent prophets taught, and, from Amos on, Israelite prophecy takes on a quite distinctive coloring. When Ezekiel speaks of "the end" that is coming upon Israel, this is surely an allusion, conscious or not, to Amos's decisive announcement of the end:

---

[2] When Jeremiah is on trial for having spoken words of judgment on Judah, some of the "elders of the land" recall that Micah had prophesied in a similar vein – but it is they, not Jeremiah, who make the connection (see Jer 26:16–19).

> The end has come upon my people Israel;
> > I will never again pass by them. (Amos 8:2)

> Thus says the Lord GOD:
> Disaster after disaster! See it comes.
> > An end has come, the end has come,
> It has awakened against you: see, it comes! (Ezek 7:5–6)

All the prophets down to the exilic period stand in a sense on the shoulders of Amos. Only with the later parts of Ezekiel and, pre-eminently, with Deutero-Isaiah, do we encounter a style of Israelite prophecy that is focused on salvation and blessing

But the history of the *explicit* reception of the book of Amos, as Robert Martin-Achard has set it out,[3] shows that many of those who quoted Amos did not do so with any awareness of his distinctive message of doom. During the Second Temple period, awareness of the individuality of the separate prophetic books seems to some extent to have been lost, and this may have been especially true of the Minor Prophets, lumped together as parts of the Book of the Twelve to the expense of their individual characteristics. This is how Ben Sira, for example, sees them, as an undifferentiated collection, all of whom prophesied blessing:

> May the bones of the Twelve Prophets
> > send forth new life from where they lie,
> for they comforted the people of Jacob
> > and delivered them with confident hope. (Sir 49:10)

Despite our modern sense of Amos (and Hosea) as particularly important figures in eighth-century Israel, Josephus does not mention them at all in his *Biblical Antiquities* – a reminder that what

---

3   Robert Martin-Achard, *Amos: l'homme, le message, l'influence* (Geneva: Labor et Fides, 1984). My discussion in this chapter is heavily dependent on Martin-Achard's book.

strikes us as important may not have seemed so in the past. Amos is also cited very little in other Jewish sources. A rare example is Tobit 2:6, where Tobit is called away from a meal to bury one of his fellow exiles, and cites Amos:

> Then I remembered the prophecy of Amos, how he said against Bethel,
>> "Your festivals shall be turned into mourning,
>> and all your songs into lamentation."

The passage is not quoted as a prophecy that has "come true" but more, I think, as a hallowed biblical phrase that perfectly fits the need of the moment. In particular, there is no sense of the original function of the saying as a threat to sinners; it is taken more as a lament for the plight into which the Jews have come.

In the New Testament, similarly, Amos is hardly used. The reference to the young man in Mark's Gospel who flees naked in the garden of Gethsemane (Mark 14:51–52) may perhaps be an allusion to Amos:

> and those who are stout of heart among the mighty
>> shall flee away naked on that day,
>>> says the LORD. (Amos 2:16)

Stephen's speech in Acts cites Amos 5:25–26 (probably following a text nearer to the LXX where the divine names are taken to mean "tent"), but substituting "Babylon" for "Damascus" in a conscious reference to the exile of the sixth century:

> "But God turned away from them and handed them over to worship the host of heaven, as it is written in the book of the prophets:
>> 'Did you offer to me slain victims and sacrifices
>>> for forty years in the wilderness, O house of Israel?
>> No, you took along the tent of Moloch,

> and the star of your god Rephan,
>   the images that you made to worship;
> so I will remove you beyond Babylon.'" (Acts 7:42–43)

This is one of the few references to "pagan" worship in Amos. We have seen that it is probably an addition to the book, making the point that the Israelites have worshipped false gods, whereas Amos himself seems to have believed that they worshipped Yʜwʜ but in the wrong way.

There is a similar use of the passage (along with Amos 9:11) in the *Damascus Document*. In a passage found only in the Cairo Geniza version, we read:

> [12] When the two houses of Israel were divided, [13] Ephraim departed from Judah. And all the apostates were given up to the sword, but those who held fast [14] escaped to the land of the north; as God said, *I will exile the tabernacle of your king* [15] *and the bases of your statues from my tent to Damascus* (Amos v, 26–27).
>
> The Books of the Law are the tabernacle [16] of the king; as God said, *I will raise up the tabernacle of David which is fallen* (Amos ix, 11). The *king* [17] is the congregation; and the *bases of the statues* are the Books of the Prophets [18] whose sayings Israel despised. The *star* is the Interpreter of the Law [19] who shall come to Damascus; as it is written, *A star shall come forth out of Jacob and a sceptre shall rise* [20] *out of Israel* (Num. xxiv, 17). The *sceptre* is the Prince of the whole congregation, and when he comes *he shall smite* [21] *all the children of Seth* (Num. xxiv, 17). (*Damascus Document* MS A VII.12b–21a)[4]

Here, what is probably in origin an oracle condemning the northern kingdom is understood positively, to refer to the restoration of the Torah alongside a new community that takes over the role of the Davidic king.

---

[4]   The translation is from Geza Vermes, *The Complete Dead Sea Scrolls in English* (New York: Allen Lane/Penguin, 1997), 133; line numbers have been added.

Acts 15:12–21 quotes in a similar vein from the epilogue to Amos – again, ironically from a modern critical perspective, since this is perhaps the least likely oracle in the book to go back to the prophet himself:

> The whole assembly kept silence, and listened to Barnabas and Paul as they told of all the signs and wonders that God had done through them among the Gentiles. After they finished speaking, James replied, "My brothers, listen to me. Simeon has related how God first looked favorably on the Gentiles, to take from among them a people for his name. This agrees with the words of the prophets, as it is written,
>
>> 'After this I will return,
>> and I will rebuild the dwelling of David, which has fallen;
>>> from its ruins I will rebuild it,
>>>> and I will set it up,
>> so that all other peoples may seek the Lord –
>>> even all the Gentiles over whom my
>>>> name has been called.
>>> Thus says the Lord, who has
>>>> been making these things
>>>> known from long ago.'
>
> Therefore I have reached the decision that we should not trouble those Gentiles who are turning to God, but we should write to them to abstain only from things polluted by idols and from fornication and from whatever has been strangled and from blood. For in every city, for generations past, Moses has had those who proclaim him, for he has been read aloud every Sabbath in the synagogues."

The same passage is cited at Qumran in *Florilegium* (4Q174), where it is treated messianically:

> [7] And concerning His words to David, *And I* [*will give*] *you* [*rest*] *from all your enemies* (2 Sam. vii, 11), this means that He will give them rest from all [8] the children of Belial who cause them to stumble so that they may be destroyed [by their errors,] just as they came with a [devilish] plan to cause the [sons] of [9] light

to stumble and to devise against them a wicked plot, that [they might become subject] to Belial in their [wicked] straying.

[10] *The Lord declares to you that He will build you a House* (2 Sam. vii, 11c). *I will raise up your seed after you* (2 Sam. vii, 12). *I will establish the throne of his kingdom* [11] *[for ever]* (2 Sam. vii, 13). *[I will be] his father and he shall be my son.* (2 Sam. vii, 14). He is the Branch of David who shall arise with the Interpreter of the Law [12] [to rule] in Zion [at the end] of time. As it is written, *I will raise up the tent of David that is fallen* (Amos ix, 11). That is to say, the fallen *tent of* [13] *David* is he who shall arise to save Israel. (4Q174 frg.1 I.7–13)[5]

The New Testament and Qumran references all show evidence of "charismatic exegesis," where biblical texts are taken to be fulfilled in the current events happening to the Christian/Qumran community.[6] Interestingly, it is the same two passages (Amos 5:25–27 and 9:11–12) that are cited both in the New Testament and at Qumran. The Christian use shows that these two texts of Amos were important for justifying both the mission to the Gentiles and the abandonment of the mission to the Jews, who are characterized by means of Amos's words as disobedient and deserving of divine punishment. But besides these, there is little evidence of Amos being read or pondered much in Early Judaism or Christianity.[7] In any case, none of these examples is a use of the *theology* of Amos in

---

5 Ibid., 493–494; line numbers have been added.
6 The expression "charismatic exegesis" appears to have been coined by David E. Aune, who defines it as follows: "the true meaning of the text concerns eschatological prophecies which the interpreter believes are being fulfilled in the events and persons connected with the religious movement to which he belongs" (*Prophecy in Early Christianity and the Ancient Mediterranean World* [Grand Rapids: Eerdmans, 1983], 133). But see also Maurya P. Horgan, *Pesharim: Qumran Interpretations of Biblical Books* (CBQMS 8; Washington, D.C.: Catholic Biblical Association of America, 1979).
7 Martin-Achard, *Amos*, makes the point that there is very little Jewish or Christian iconography of Amos, other than as simply one of the twelve minor prophets.

any obvious sense, and they draw only on those parts of the book's message that are least likely to reflect the prophet's own distinctive thought.

In sum, it does not seem that the book of Amos was very important for the first Christians: certainly, it had none of the centrality that it has acquired in modern scholarship, and one can hardly imagine a Christian of the first few generations writing a commentary on it.

AMOS IN RABBINIC JUDAISM AND THE CHRISTIAN FATHERS

There is nevertheless a thin line of reception of the book, though seldom regarding its *distinctive* message, in Judaism and Christianity through subsequent centuries. Rabbinic texts present Amos as a rich man – against the modern tendency to see him as a "simple shepherd," but in keeping with more recent scholarly suggestions that he was a sheep breeder.[8] These texts also portray him as hesitant in speech, no doubt by analogy with Moses. This is linked to a play on Amos's name, which is taken to mean "heavy (of tongue)." His death was variously described, one theory being that he was assassinated by Uzziah – it is hard to see why this should have happened – or, more plausibly, by Amaziah, the priest of Bethel, and his son.[9] But there is little reflection in the rabbis on Amos's teaching as opposed to his biography. Though elements of his teaching are

---

[8] See Midrash Leviticus Rabbah §6 (Martin-Achard, *Amos*, 187); cf. *b. Nedarim* 38a. Martin-Achard's source for most of his references is Malke Blechmann, *Das Buch Amos in Talmud und Midrasch* (Leipzig: O. Schmidt, 1937).

[9] The Christian pseudepigraph, the *Lives of the Prophets* (which may have Jewish roots), treats Amos as one of the six prophets who were martyred, the others being Micah, Isaiah, Jeremiah, Ezekiel, and Zechariah son of Jehoiada.

referred back to incidents in the Torah, Amos as an eighth-century prophet is never clearly in focus. Thus "they have sold the righteous for silver, and the needy for a pair of sandals" is taken as a reference to Joseph's brothers selling him into slavery, rather than to exploitation of the poor in the time of Amos himself.[10]

At other times, Amos's specific predictions of doom are taken as statements of general principle, and in a way almost certainly alien to the thinking of the prophet himself. An example is a rabbinic treatment of Amos 3:2 ("You only have I known of all the families of the earth, therefore I will punish you for all your iniquities") in the Babylonian Talmud, *Avodah Zarah* 4a. Rabbi Abahu, expounding this verse, tells the parable of a man who had two debtors, one his friend and the other his enemy. He made the first, the friend, refund the debt by continual, regular payments, whereas the second, the enemy, he forced to discharge the debt in one big payment. The meaning of the parable is that Israel pays off its guilt to God by its continual suffering, whereas the nations are punished comprehensively all at once. This implies (a point drawn out in Genesis Rabbah) that Israel though continually punished is never destroyed, whereas other nations may be annihilated for their sins. Thus God's slow but steady punishment of Israel is a sign of his love for his own people. This is probably just about the opposite of what Amos meant, but it integrates his teaching into a systematic account of divine providence and retribution.[11] A similar theme is read out of (or rather read into) Amos 5:18–19, where the notion of the day of YHWH being darkness is said to hold true primarily for the Gentiles, not Israel.

---

[10] See Martin-Achard, *Amos*, 189, with reference to Pirqe R. Eliezer §38, Tanhuma Noah §4, and other texts. The brothers each bought a pair of sandals with the money they acquired from selling Joseph.

[11] Martin-Achard, *Amos*, 189–190.

A further example where Amos's teaching is in effect inverted in rabbinic interpretation is the treatment of Amos 9:7:

> Are you not like the Ethiopians to me,
>   O people of Israel? says the LORD.
> Did I not bring up Israel from the land of Egypt,
>   And the Philistines from Caphtor and the Arameans from Kir?

As we have seen, this probably means that the Israelites are no better than the Cushites in YHWH's eyes, and is about the strongest statement anywhere in the Bible that Israel is *not* God's chosen people. Rabbinic reading argues that Amos was reminding his hearers that Cushites differ from all other nations (because of the color of their skin) and arguing that Israel similarly is different from all others because of the just way they behave.[12] That is why they are compared to the Cushites.

There is an interesting rabbinic treatment of Amos 5:4, "seek me and live," within a context of the discussion of how many commandments there are in the Torah. According to Rabbi Simla (ca. 260 CE), Moses revealed 613 commandments, as normally reckoned in rabbinic Judaism. But David reduced them to eleven (see Psalm 15), Micah to three (Micah 6:8), and Isaiah to two (Isa 56:1), and then finally Amos summed them up in one single command, "seek me and live."[13] Here, Amos is seen, as the prophets generally are in rabbinic Judaism, as teachers of Torah, but there is an awareness that the prophet called for a single-minded adherence to YHWH – though there is no thought that the 613 separate commandments were therefore *not* meant to be kept exactly. Amos's moral exhortation is also recalled in a saying of Rabbi Ashi, who is

---

[12] Pirqe R. Eliezer §53; see Martin-Achard, *Amos*, 196–197.
[13] Martin-Achard, *Amos*, 192. Note the variant in which Amos reduced them to two and Habakkuk to one (Hab 2:4).

said to have wept every time he read Amos 5:15 because it says that even if God is truly sought, it only *may be* that he will be gracious to the remnant of Joseph, so that Israel cannot be sure of the grace of God even if they zealously obey the law – which is probably an idea that Amos truly had.

As Martin-Achard points out, the ethical content of Amos is far from lacking in rabbinic interpretation, but the tragic note, the threat of complete and irrevocable destruction, has disappeared, as has the questioning of Israel's special status. Traditional Christian interpretation has also usually failed to see the final "no!" in this prophetic book. In fact, comparatively little use is made of Amos in patristic literature, though there are commentaries by Cyril of Alexandria, Theodoret, and Theodore of Mopsuestia – so from both Alexandrian and Antiochene traditions. But the oracles of final judgment on sin are barely discussed by the Fathers, though the condemnations of sin in themselves are noticed. As with the Jewish exegetical tradition, what modern interpreters see as the central message of Amos is not at all at the center of interest. Amos 4:13 was of particular concern because it taught that the one God is the creator of the world:

> For lo, the one who forms the mountains, creates the wind,
>> reveals his thoughts to mortals,
> makes the morning darkness,
>> and treads on the heights of the earth –
>> the Lord, the God of hosts, is his name!

This passage could be seen as having force against various forms of Gnosticism, with their denial that the true God was the creator; while in the clause "declaring to man his thought" (NRSV: "reveals his thought to mortals"), the last two words are rendered in the LXX with *ton christon autou* ("his anointed one/messiah/ Christ") – a mistake by the Greek translators – and so were taken to be a Christological reference. Tertullian so argued from the Latin version (*annuntiante in homines Christum suum*: "declaring unto man His Christ"), as did Augustine in the *City of God* (*adnuntians in hominibus Christum suum*: "announcing to men His Christ").[14] Jerome, on the other hand, correctly saw that the Hebrew did not have this sense. Given that the verse also contains a reference to the "spirit" (*pneuma*), it was possible to find here a proof text for the doctrine of the Trinity. But this became an embarrassment during the Arian controversy, since it appears to affirm that the *pneuma* was created: Athanasius accordingly argued that its meaning here was simply "wind," basing this on the absence of the definite article, and in this he was undoubtedly right, as Jerome also argued on the basis of the Hebrew text. This does remind us, however, how much the Fathers read the Old Testament in general for doctrinal reasons, and how little interested they were in the theology of the books taken on their own terms, which modern biblical study has striven to elucidate.

AMOS IN THE TEACHING OF SAVONAROLA

Ludwig Markert and Robert Martin-Achard have established that there is one considerable figure in the history of the Church who did take seriously the ethical and eschatological message we have seen to be central both to the prophet himself and to the book that left the hands of the final redactors.[15] This is the Dominican

---

[14] Ibid., 204. See Tertullian, *adversus Marcionem* 3:6:6 (where the quotation is said to be from Joel); and Augustine *de civitate Dei* 15:18. Augustine in fact cites Amos extremely rarely, though he does read the epilogue Christologically, seeing Jesus as the new representative of the line of David.

[15] Ludwig Markert, "Amos, Amosbuch' *TRE* 2:482–485; Martin-Achard, *Amos*, 213–219. For a recent full discussion of Savonarola's use of Amos, see Andrew Mein, "The Radical Amos in Savonarola's Florence," in *Aspects of Amos: Exegesis and Interpretation* (eds. A. C. Hagedorn and A. Mein; LHBOTS 536; London: T & T Clark, 2011), 117–140.

friar Girolamo Savonarola (1452–1498), who preached a series of sermons on Amos and Zechariah in Florence during Lent 1496. His identification of the people condemned by Amos with the ecclesiastical and civic authorities of his day was a factor leading to his eventual arrest, trial, and execution the following year. For example, he identified Amos's "cows of Bashan" with the concubines of priests and rulers, and says that priests say Mass the morning after they have spent the night with these concubines. Here are some typical excerpts from Savonarola's sermons, in which the parallels with Amos's argumentation are as apparent as the actual quotations from his book:

> Italy is unwilling to believe: Italy, you have been told and warned many times: I have told you from God, Italy, I have told you to do penance. Rome, I have told you to do penance; Milan, I have told you to do penance; Venice, I have told you to do penance. I have told all the wise men of the world that there is no remedy except penance, but you are unwilling to believe, unwilling to open your ears; you mock. That is why God says, I detest your pride and I hate your houses, which will be burned and destroyed, and you will go into the house of the devil. Italy, you are unwilling to believe; all you do is to say "Amos was speaking of his own time; his message does not concern our times!" But I tell you that Amos will come true in this present time …
>
> Oh, how many will have to die, how many will have to go to hell! Let everyone prepare: *Quia ecce mandabit Deus et percutiet domum maiorem ruinis et domum minorem scissionibus* ["For behold God will command, and he will strike the larger house with ruins and the smaller house with divisions"]; Amos says that both the large and the small house will be ruined – by "the large house" he means Israel, and by "the small house" the region of Judah. Both were annihilated and destroyed by the Assyrians and by Nebuchadnezzar. By "the large house" we understand the clergy, and by "the small house" we understand the people. So the Saviour says, "I will strike these houses and destroy them." O house of Israel, O "large house," listen to me, lend me your ear, believe me; I would not cry out so much if I did not know what

I am talking about. You should believe me, for I tell you that you will have to flee from the sword. The Saviour threatens Rome, and threatens the clergy.... If Rome and Italy do penance, the evil I am announcing will not happen, but if they do not repent, all that I am foretelling will take place, because there is no cure but penitence. Well, my brother, what do you think? Do you think they will repent? I tell you the truth: I do not believe it.[16]

Savonarola draws on Amos's condemnation of sacrifice to attack the reduction of religion to external ceremonies in the absence of justice and probity: "you have changed good deeds into wormwood, that is, into ceremonies and bad examples."[17] He presents what Martin-Achard calls "une explication actualisante" of the text: an interpretation that applies it to present circumstances (i.e., *actualizes* it). But in the process, it is clear that Savonarola has grasped what the text was about in its own day, however different in details Amos's situation was from fifteen-century Florence. The corruption of religion is the common denominator in both cases. And, like Amos, Savonarola probably did not expect to be listened to, and was probably not surprised when his reward was martyrdom.

AMOS DURING THE REFORMATION AND IN CRITICAL SCHOLARSHIP

Later, Martin Luther similarly presented himself as Amos-like: a simple man addressing the leaders of the Church and condemning "false sanctity." He argued that Amos, like the other Minor Prophets, had a dialectical relationship with the religious traditions

---

[16] Martin-Achard, *Amos*, 213–224; this is my translation of his French version of the original Italian, from Savonarola, *Prediche italiane ai fiorentini (1494–1496)* (3 vols.; ed. R. Palmarocchi; Perugia, Venezia, 1930–1935), 3:453–458.

[17] Martin-Achard, *Amos*, 217.

of Israel, accepting that Israel was chosen by God yet grasping that God was now challenging that special relationship because of the people's sin. In this, we see something of a return to the original intentions of the prophet, rather than the typical patristic Christological interpretation (which Luther nonetheless continued to support, as can be seen from his messianic exegesis of the epilogue). Luther gives his interpretation a characteristic twist: it is by faith that Israel was called to "seek God," not by "works." Amos 5 (which, as we saw, is in many ways the core of the book) particularly conveys what Luther understood as this Gospel challenge. That "justice will flow down like water," for example, means that the righteousness God gives to those who have faith is irresistible, not a matter of their own merits, and it is the righteousness that comes from God, not from the law.

John Calvin wrote a complete commentary on Amos.[18] Regarding Amos 3:2, Calvin argues, as one might expect, that the choice of Israel was an act of pure divine grace and that it makes Israel even more culpable than any other people – this seems to be more or less what Amos was actually saying. Calvin stresses the providence of God in the governance of the world, and argues that God's judgment is meant to lead human beings to repentance. Amos's calls to repentance are therefore not regarded as empty but as very seriously intended. Calvin makes much of the *Unheilsgeschichte* in Amos 4, where smaller punishments are meant to alert the people to a recognition of their sinfulness, and so bring about their reformation. On the calls to repentance in Amos 5, however, Calvin argues the case for predestination: the call to repent here serves only to increase the guilt of the unrepentant and to confirm their

---

[18] See John Calvin, *A Commentary on the Twelve Minor Prophets*, Vol. 2 (Edinburgh: Banner of Truth Trust, 1986).

damnation. Striving to be true to the plain meaning of what the prophet is saying, he stresses the possibility of repentance, but true to his own doctrine, he argues that some are already predetermined by God's decision to reject the call. This obviously goes beyond Amos's own message, but it does fairly correspond to the element of tragedy and hopelessness that we have seen to characterize the prophet's theology. Amos is hardly optimistic about the likelihood that sinners will repent and be pardoned.

Predictably, Calvin sees the sin of Israel as consisting mostly in "superstition" and vain ceremonies, but thinks that these often served to cover up injustice and oppression, the latter of which again seems close to the spirit of the prophet himself – hypocrisy lies very near to the center of the people's sin. Martin-Achard makes the valuable point that, for Calvin, it is the political leaders who are in focus in Amos, whereas the prophet himself probably envisioned a wider group – all those who were profiting from the prosperity made possible by the successful reign of Jeroboam II and the quiescence of major world powers. So, for Calvin, the message is above all *political*, whereas for Amos and his circle it was *social*. And where Amos condemned concrete bad practices, Calvin focuses on the underlying attitude of the leaders – a more overtly theological analysis of contemporary problems. Like so many before and since, Calvin looked to produce a systematic theology in his exposition of the prophet's book, whereas the theology of Amos himself was more occasional, driven by the exigencies of the moment.

Nevertheless Calvin's commentary is fair to the main lines of Amos's message in concentrating on the themes of sin and judgment and relegating the "messianic" epilogue (though of course he thought it authentic) to an appendix in his commentary. More than most readers of the prophets in the past, Calvin had a real concern with the book's meaning in its original context, though, like Savonarola, he drew frequent parallels between the prophet's context and his own. That has always been normal in reading the Bible in the Church, and it continues to be so even in the historical-critical tradition, where there is no doubt a greater awareness of the distance between ourselves and the biblical writers, but still an ongoing concern for the *application* of the text to the needs of the current situation.

Nevertheless, critical reading of the prophets produced a fresh awareness of both the original angularity and yet also of the possible contemporary relevance of Amos, to a greater extent than ever before. Since the groundbreaking work of Bernhard Duhm, biblical scholars have sought to reestablish the original message of Amos,[19] and have found it to lie in a prescience about coming divine judgment that is inextricably linked with the analysis of contemporary society – a society in which assiduous religious observance masks deep social injustices – as flawed. In the early twentieth century, this led to a rather optimistic perception that the prophets spoke of "the fatherhood of God and the brotherhood of man," and taught "ethical monotheism." But toward the end of the century, the prophetic message – and especially that of Amos – began to be heard again in its sharpness and vehemence through the work of liberation theologians, especially in South America.

AMOS IN LIBERATION THEOLOGY

Liberation theology is well known for its use of the theme of the exodus as a symbol of liberation from oppression. But it also uses

---

[19] Bernhard Duhm, *Israels Propheten* (Tübingen: J. C. B. Mohr [Paul Siebeck], 1916).

the prophets, and among them Amos is of special importance because of his obvious attacks on the rulers and the rich in his day.[20] It was not felt to be a stretch to apply this message to the situation in many South American countries, where the poor systematically were exploited and the rich did very much as they pleased. What is more, the traditional church authorities had for long been associated with the ruling classes, and so it was natural to mobilize Amos's condemnations of the religious establishment and the system of sacrifice and festivals to declare a judgment from God on the church in its traditional forms (not all that different from Savonarola's attacks in Florence). Liberation theologians criticized the collaboration of church and state to oppress the poor in the light of a text that both church and state recognized as authoritative, the book of Amos. Here was a "religious" thinker who criticized "religion" in the name of the God that very religion failed to honor.

There is a striking "rewriting" of Amos by Roger Parmentier, in which the oracles on the nations are recast to refer to the generals and other rulers in South America, but also in European nations.[21]

---

[20] Though interestingly, *The Cambridge Companion to Liberation Theology* (ed. C. Rowland; Cambridge: Cambridge University Press, 1999) has only one reference to Amos, in the chapter "Liberation and Reconstruction" by Charles Villa-Vicencio: "the biblical God is never revealed in a neutral place (whether in the mind of intellectuals or among the counsellors of the Pharaohs or high priests), but among the slaves (Exodus), the peasant farmers (Amos), the widows and orphans (New Testament)" (166). But see the fuller works by Carol J. Dempsey, *The Prophets: A Liberation-Critical Reading* (Minneapolis: Augsburg Fortress, 2000) and Anthony R. Ceresko's *Introduction to the Old Testament: A Liberation Perspective* (rev. ed.; Maryknoll: Orbis, 2001).

[21] Roger Parmentier, "Amos réécrit pour 1978," in idem, *Actualisations de la Bible: Osée, Amos, Jonas, Habaquq, Cantique des Cantiques, Jacques, 1 Thessaloniciens, Luc 15* (Paris: Editions Karthala, 1982), 49–70. Further details may be found in Martin-Achard, *Amos*, 260–265.

But the main liberation theologian to draw on Amos is probably Carlos Mesters in Brazil, who proposed four theses about how the message of Amos can be applied to the present state of the poor in Latin America.[22] First, he argues that Amos grasped the historical reality of his people and took up a mission toward them in the light of the divine plan. Amos saw the prosperity of the northern kingdom as the result of exploitation of the poor by the rich, and was moved by this to give up his home in Tekoa, in the south, and move north in order to denounce the disorder in northern society. The parallels to the situation in Latin America, and the need for the Church to speak out against abuse, are all too clear.

Second, Mesters says that, in the light of God's word, Amos sees the contradictions within the current reality of God's people. The people who were released from slavery in Egypt have fallen back into bondage, and that to their own fellow-countrymen; the assiduous cultic life in the north only papers over the social exploitation. The contemporary parallels Mesters notes are again only all too obvious, and he refers to various official Catholic documents on social justice, which the leaders in South America are ignoring.

Third, Amos's stance on God's side against the structures of sin means that he is a permanent goad to those in power. Amos paid dearly for his activity on behalf of the poor, being expelled from the northern kingdom. It is for modern prophets, such as Mesters himself, to oppose exploitation and false power. Peace can exist only as the fruit of justice, otherwise it is a false peace.

Fourth, however – and here we note that Mesters does not ignore the epilogue – there can be hope because God has purposes that

---

[22] Carlos Mesters in a pamphlet produced by the Centro de Estudos Biblicos (CEBI) in Rio de Janeiro and supplied to Martin-Achard, from whose work (*Amos*, 266–269), I have taken the following summary.

exceed those of sinful humanity, though this thesis is developed more in connection with Hosea than with Amos.

It is noteworthy that Mesters's reading rests on historical-critical perceptions about what Amos did and said in his own time, and so Mesters is interested in Amos as an historical figure. To be sure, Mesters presupposes that Amos was a preacher of repentance, which as we have seen is disputed in critical circles. But the parallels that Mesters draws with contemporary society in the countries he knows best are far from artificial and bear witness to the power of this prophetic book to continue to challenge and to act as a thorn in the flesh of the rich and powerful.

The exodus has remained a more central theme in liberation theology than the teaching of the prophets, but it is clear that a prophet such as Amos has much to contribute to the struggle for human liberation. Though the prophet himself may have been utterly pessimistic about the future of what he saw as a thoroughly rotten society, his book retains elements of hope, and these have been able to inspire liberation theologians with the idea that, even out of the desolation of the human spirit in South America, God may still be able to bring healing and restoration of the rights of the downtrodden.

CHAPTER 7

The Theology of Amos Then and Now

There are two ways of regarding the relationship between the theology of the book of Amos and our own theological thinking. One is the "canonical" way. Here, we interpret the book explicitly from a faith position, and seek to integrate its theology into a pan-biblical theology, which is also consistent with Christian faith as we understand it. We have seen, in Chapter 5, that this is a perfectly possible route to understanding the book. The problem with it is that it becomes difficult to hear the book as saying anything differ-ent, or at least radically different, from what we already believe on other grounds. It takes its place within the canon of Scripture as a partial witness to Christian truth, and needs to be read within (and constrained by) that matrix.

The alternative is to think about the book's theology as it emerges from a relatively uncommitted examination, and to ask whether that theology has anything still to contribute to modern theolog-ical thinking. This alternative route is open to the criticism that it is not how the faith community ever read Scripture in the past. Amos was never understood by past generations of Christians on the basis of what could be reconstructed of the book's theology by historical-critical methods, but only as part of canonical Scripture. Once we detach it from that context, then the question arises why we should be interested in its theology anyway. It becomes simply an old religious text, and probably a not very important one.

The reader will have seen by now that this book is written on the basis that the "original" meaning of the book, and even the original meaning of the prophet himself in so far as this differs from the impression made by the completed book, is important for theology. The fact that the book is recognized as canonical forces us to consider it seriously, but does not in itself tell us how we are meant to interpret it. And even if the book were not canonical, it remains a witness to a very early phase in the theological thinking of ancient Israel, of which modern Judaism and Christianity are lineal descendants. The book of Amos is at least as important as the works of the rabbis or Church Fathers, as evidence for the way in which God was thought about at an early stage of theological reflection within the tradition that has become the inheritance of Christians and Jews today.

Accordingly, I will try in this chapter to take the theology of Amos and his book, as far as we can reconstruct them, and ask how they might be assimilated or challenged in the light of more recent theological insights. There is a certain paradox or circularity here because Amos is, at one and the same time, one of the sources of later Jewish and Christian theological ideas and yet a text that those theological ideas may need to challenge. Our current theological thinking is different from his, yet probably would not exist without his reflection on the nature and purposes of God (and that of many other prophets and writers, of course). Just as people differ from and may need to challenge their parents yet would not be the people they are without them (for good or ill), so a modern Christian or Jew may need to criticize certain features of the theology of Amos yet needs to acknowledge that neither Christianity nor Judaism would be what they are without his remarkable ideas.

As I said earlier in this book, Amos was, after all, Israel's first theologian.

THE IDEA OF GOD

The God of the book of Amos is presented in rather anthropomorphic terms, for example as "standing beside" the altar (9:1) or as sieving the nation (9:9). But in general, it seems clear that these are metaphors and were understood as such both by the editors of the book and by the prophet himself. For though God can be "seen," at least by the prophet, God is also ubiquitous, present (against some other Israelite traditions), even in Sheol and at the bottom of the sea. He exercises control over all the nations. As we have seen, this latter idea seems to have been shared by both Amos and his hearers, which implies that Israel already believed in something that was approaching monotheism even before Amos himself. We know from archaeological evidence that deities besides YHWH were worshipped in Israel at the time of Amos, yet the conception of God that emerges from the book treats YHWH as the only God with whom both Israel and foreign nations have to deal. This is not exactly "monotheism" as conceived in later philosophical theology – it is not an answer to the question "Is the divine one or many?" It is an exaltation of YHWH, the God of Israel, as supreme over the whole world. In this sense, religions throughout the ancient Near East can be said to have monotheistic tendencies, in that despite worshipping a multitude of gods, people tended to regard one of them as the ruler of all, and to think that this god controlled the fates of all nations.[1] It was normal in the ancient

---

[1]   Such tendencies do not arrive at the monotheism found in later Judaism and Christianity, but are more like what is sometimes called "henotheism" – the worship of one main or preferred god.

world, for example, to believe that gods could hear one's prayers anywhere and everywhere, and to believe that the gods were all-seeing and all-controlling. So perhaps Israel was not very distinctive in this respect.

Yet already in Amos, we seem to have a belief that goes beyond this common ancient Near Eastern theology. In the oracles against the nations, YHWH is famously concerned even with the relations between non-Israelite nations (Amos 2:1). There are even hints, as we have seen, that YHWH is the God of all the world and *not* specially the God of Israel (9:7), which is an idea that occurs little in the pages of the Old Testament or in Israelite and Jewish theology.[2] God may be conceived of as "physical" in some special sense – there is no evidence for a "purely spiritual" conception of God at this stage, or perhaps ever in ancient Israel[3] – but he has a means of acting within world history that implies a kind of all-pervasive presence and concern. Certainly, YHWH is nothing like the image of Baal mocked by Elijah in 1 Kings, a god who may be unable to hear because "either he is meditating, or he has wandered away, or he is on a journey, or perhaps he is asleep and must be wakened" (1 Kgs 18:27). It may be true to say that this is a caricature of how

---

[2] For examples where YHWH is believed to have directed the affairs of other nations, see Deuteronomy 2 and Patrick D. Miller, "God's Other Stories: On the Margins of Deuteronomic Theology," in *Realia Dei: Essays in Archaeology and Biblical Interpretation in Honor of Edward F. Campbell Jr. at His Retirement* (eds. Prescott H. Williams, Jr. and Theodore Hiebert; Atlanta: Scholars Press, 1999), 185–194, reprinted in idem, *Israelite Religion and Biblical Theology: Collected Essays* (JSOTSup 267; Sheffield: Sheffield Academic Press, 2000), 593–602; also Brent A. Strawn, "Deuteronomy," in *Theological Bible Commentary* (eds. Gail R. O'Day and David L. Petersen; Louisville: Westminster John Knox, 2009), 66–67.

[3] See the important discussion in Benjamin D. Sommer, *The Bodies of God and the World of Ancient Israel* (Cambridge: Cambridge University Press, 2009).

the gods were conceived in other nations, but there is no doubt that the God of Amos at least is very far from such a conception.

The God of the book of Amos is not only concerned with nations and their history, but is also active in the natural world. In the "doxologies," he is presented as controlling the elements, making the sun rise and set and pouring water on the earth. There is clearly no opposition or tension between YHWH as the god of history and other gods as gods of nature, such as many biblical theologians believed in during the middle years of the twentieth century. Like all ancient Near Eastern gods, YHWH is active in both the "natural" and the "political" spheres.[4] His judgment expresses itself both through military invasion and through earthquakes, famine, and drought.

What is remarkable about YHWH is that in neither sphere is he necessarily benevolent toward Israel: natural forces can be hostile under the guidance of the one who "darkens the day into night … [and] makes destruction flash out against the strong" (5:8–9), and he can pursue his own nation just as much as other nations. It looks as if these are possibilities that Amos's audience had not considered; evidently, they regarded YHWH as omnibenevolent toward them and welcomed the "day of YHWH" that they were expecting as a day of light. It was not unheard of in the ancient Near East for gods to act in a hostile way toward their people – compare the Mesha stele, where "as for Omri, king of Israel, he humbled Moab many days for Chemosh was angry at his land."[5] But there does not seem to be any precise ancient Near Eastern parallel for the idea

---

4 This was decisively demonstrated to be true both of YHWH and of other ancient Near Eastern gods in B. Albrektson, *History and the Gods: An Essay on the Idea of Historical Events as Divine Manifestations in the Ancient Near East and in Israel* (ConBOT 1; Lund: Gleerup, 1967).

5 *ANET*, 320 (cited more fully in chapter 2 at note 6).

found in Amos that YHWH is actually going to *destroy* Israel and annul his relationship with his chosen people altogether.

Israel's relationship with YHWH becomes conflicted from the time of Amos onwards, with a popular assumption that "YHWH is the God of Israel and Israel is the people of YHWH" and that God is Israel's "helper" (again, as Julius Wellhausen put it)[6] coming to clash with the prophetic message that "the end has come upon my people Israel" (Amos 8:2). From the time of Amos onwards, the YHWH–Israel relationship will never again be simple and reassuring, but always prone to dialectic. This is in one way a consequence of Amos's monotheism, because there are no hostile gods to whom opposition to Israel can be attributed; in another way, perhaps it is also one of the precursors of a later, more theorized monotheism, since it removes any sense that YHWH depends on Israel in some way, and it gives him the sovereign freedom that is a precondition of full monotheistic belief – a freedom that in much later times would become a belief in "omnipotence" (itself a complicated notion).

How far can we say that Amos or the editors of his book believed in the same God that modern Jews or Christians worship? To answer this, we would first have to decide how the God of Jews and Christians is generally conceived, and we would have to allow for difference both between and within these two religious traditions. There is no single Jewish or Christian notion of God, and there is no "Judaeo-Christian tradition" that unites the two religions. Seen from within, moreover, they are very different from each other. Yet there are important features that are shared, and these certainly include an idea of divine freedom from external constraint that is clearly part of the message of Amos, together

---

[6]   See chapter 2 note 2 above.

with a recognition that God's commitment to his people (whoever exactly "his people" is understood to designate, a point on which Jews and Christians tend to differ) is not to be presumed upon or taken for granted. For all their diversity, the religious beliefs of Amos, his editors, later Jews, and later Christians agree on the dialectical character of the divine–human relationship – it is not a relationship that can be relaxed into, as a kind of comfort blanket, but one that constantly and consistently *challenges* human beings. Amos stands at the head of this tradition, questioning the complacent religion of his day.

CORPORATE AND INDIVIDUAL IDENTITY

Most commentators agree that one of the radical ideas in Amos is the prediction that the whole nation will perish for the sins of a few.[7] By their misdemeanors, the ruling classes and the rich call down upon themselves the anger of Yhwh, but this anger expresses itself in the destruction of the nation *as a whole*, not just of the guilty parties. Later editors toned down this idea, insisting that it is the "sinners of my people" who will die (9:10), but it looks as though Amos himself believed in collective punishment. In the past, it was often argued that it was not until the time of Jeremiah and Ezekiel that the idea of a discriminating judgment arose, and that "individualism" only then replaced collective responsibility in popular consciousness. (The postexilic period was then seen as the time when individualism in religion flourished, producing among other effects the whole of the wisdom literature.) But most scholars now doubt whether there is any simplistic progression from

---

[7] Again, see Abraham J. Heschel, *The Prophets* (New York: Perennial Classics, 2001 [orig: 1962]), esp. 17–19 ("Few Are Guilty, All Are Responsible").

corporate to individual ways of thinking, since individual and collective responsibility can be found in all periods and, indeed, are both still with us today.[8] The study of Amos certainly calls any such hypothetical progression into question, since if his message of total destruction was radical and challenging, that must mean that his audience would not have expected divine judgment to have a collective character: hence, they must have already been, in some sense, "individualists." Later individualism, so far as it existed, must have been the reassertion of old beliefs rather than the development of new ones – rather like later belief in the "day of YHWH" as a time of blessing for Israel was a reassertion of what most people believed about it before Amos.

We might say on this issue that Amos was simply a realist. Ancient warfare did not discriminate between innocent and guilty, nor did (or do) earthquakes. The idea that YHWH might "sieve" the nation and destroy only the guilty (Amos 9:9), like the idea in Ezekiel 9:4 that he might find a way to mark the righteous so that the angel of death would pass them by, is in practice wishful thinking. But of course, what actually happens in time of war or natural disaster raises huge problems about the justice of God, and this takes us into the whole area designated as "theodicy" in modern theology since the time of Leibniz. Can Amos, read on its own terms, contribute to this huge philosophical and theological debate?

The book already presents us with two different ideas: the indiscriminate judgment Amos himself seems to have believed in and the "sieving" form of divine visitation held by the book's editors. The latter stresses divine justice but is unrealistic; the former asserts

---

[8] See the classic discussion by J. W. Rogerson, "The Hebrew Conception of Corporate Personality," *JTS* 21 (1970): 1–16.

justice on God's part yet seems to deny it in practice. Nothing is gained by a "canonical" attempt to reconcile these two approaches or to integrate them into some larger framework – both are still on the table for debate in the present. The prophets in general seem utterly obsessed with the issue of God's justice, and both they and their editors sought to avoid any way of thinking that called divine justice into question. As I argued earlier, it seems as though Amos's moral condemnations of Israel are probably part of his drive to produce a theodicy, rather than being veiled moral exhortations. The point of his message is not "repent!" – it is already too late for that – but "give glory to YHWH" (cf. Josh 7:19; Job 2:9), that is, accept your guilt and confess that the coming disasters are fully justified. The issue of corporate versus individual responsibility arises within this context, not in its own right. It is part of the larger question, "Is God just?"

Only in Job is this question, possibly, answered in the negative. In the prophets, on the contrary, there is a great emphasis on its positive answer. The justice of God is for them a given, and other pieces on the theological chessboard have to be moved round to make sure that it is not displaced. In the modern context, the question of God's justice still arises and causes anguish for many people. While a canonical approach to the Bible would urge that the witness of the book of Amos should not be heard except in a context defined by other (later) testimony, such as that of prophets like Jeremiah, the book of Job, and, of course, for a Christian, the sufferings of Jesus as interpreted both by himself and by the New Testament writers, the approach we are following here suggests that it is legitimate to contemplate the book of Amos on its own terms and to ask how satisfying its message is. It seems to me that it confronts us with the question of how far we do indeed take the justice of God as the given in our deliberations, or how far we take our understanding of the empirical evidence about human suffering and guilt or innocence as the lodestone, and then try to comprehend how far we can believe in a just God. Amos is not the Bible's last word on the subject, but it is one distinctive and compelling word, and deserves to be wrestled with.

COVENANT

As we have seen, the book of Amos does not use the word *bĕrît* (ברית) to refer to the relationship between God and Israel: it occurs only in the oracles against the nations in its non-theological usage to mean "treaty" in the "covenant of brothers [NRSV: 'kinship']" at 1:9. Nevertheless, I have argued that the theological use, in which it refers to a putative contract between YHWH and Israel, is implied in Amos's own teaching. For him, the YHWH–Israel relationship is surely seen as contractual. Israel is obliged to act in certain ways, and in the case of breach of contract, YHWH will be justified in bringing about Israel's destruction. If, as Hadjiev argues, Amos 9:7 is the original message of Amos, then the prophet himself actually denied that there was any special relationship between YHWH and Israel, and hence could not have seen the relationship as contractual, since there was no relationship anyway. By the time 3:2 was written (and I have argued that this also may be by Amos himself), it had come to be seen that there was a special relationship, but, contrary to what people at large supposed, this entailed moral obligation rather than indemnity against prosecution.

The idea of a national contract with the god seems to have been an original idea of Israel's as against its ancient Near Eastern background, and if Amos was its creator then that already gives him a significant role in ancient theology. The use of *bĕrît* to express the contract implies that it was conceived on analogy with the vassal treaties that came to be known in Israel from the Assyrian period of the seventh century onwards (the older belief that Hittite treaties of the second millennium were the model is no longer widely held).[9] Amos stands just before this period began, and since he does not use the term *bĕrît* for the relationship between Yhwh and Israel, we cannot be sure that there was for him an analogy with political treaties. For him, the Yhwh–Israel contract may have been modeled on commercial contracts, in which each partner has to keep his side of a bargain. If so, this would be in line with his great interest in commercial matters. Whatever the origin of the idea, it is clear that the divine–human relationship *is* contractual, and it is equally clear that the audience does not seem to have seen matters in this way, or to have been familiar with understanding the relation of God to his human creation as a matter of mutual choice rather than of nature. It is not until the book of Deuteronomy that we find a fully worked-out expression of the theological theory involved. In Amos, the concept is only inchoate.

For a modern reader, there is a question about whether God can be conceived of as having a special relationship with just one people or nation – even a relationship as conflicted as that between Yhwh and Israel – like the book of Amos presents it. Is monotheism compatible with God having a special interest in just one group of people? The issue arises both for Judaism and for Christianity, since each in its own way has spoken of God as related uniquely or specially to itself. In both religions, there is also a strong stream of universalism – a belief that God is also concerned with the whole human race. But particularism cannot be expunged from either faith. In the eighteenth century, David Hume already saw the

---

9   See the discussion in Ernest W. Nicholson, *God and His People: Covenant and Theology in the Old Testament* (Oxford: Clarendon Press, 1986).

difficulties in a monotheism that regards God both as concerned with the whole creation and at the same time having a special interest in one group, or indeed in individual people, and he argued by implication that Judaeo-Christian monotheism was incoherent.[10] This may be one of the greatest challenges to a "biblical faith" of either the Jewish or the Christian kind. Is it thinkable that the God who created the whole universe also entered into a contractual relationship with one particular group of people?

For the Old Testament writers, this is not a problem. Amos may have rejected the idea, but he did not do so on the grounds of its philosophical incoherence; rather, he did so because he thought Israel was unworthy of the role of covenant partner for YHWH. Subsequent editors of the book clearly accepted the idea, however, even though they probably followed the prophet himself in thinking that, if there was indeed a special relationship, it conferred obligations rather than entitlements. But Hume's challenge cannot be evaded by a modern Christian or Jew. It can be countered by an appeal to the freedom and omnipotence of God: if the God monotheism believes in chooses to single out one group of people for special attention (whether to confer favors on them or to impose obligations), he is entirely free to do so. To some, however, the idea will seem like a leftover from an earlier, more "tribal" view of God.

If problems arise regarding how the universal God can relate specifically to one people or group, there is even more difficulty in seeing such a deity relating to specific *individuals*. As we have seen, Amos himself and his editors may have had rather different ideas about this, with Amos seeing Israel as a collective to be punished as a whole, whereas later editors thought of God as

[10] See Simon Blackburn, *How to Read Hume* (London: Granta, 2008), esp. 82–94.

distinguishing between the good and the evil within the nation, rewarding or punishing them appropriately according to their individual deserts. But in both cases, it is the actions of individuals that call down the divine anger, whether that affects only themselves or the whole nation of which they form part. Amos, like all the Old Testament writers, is convinced that God is aware of and reacts to what each and every person on earth does. Yhwh is both a universal God and, at the same time, the personal god of each individual, at least of each individual Israelite. This was probably unusual in the ancient Near Eastern context, where, alongside the high gods who ruled the natural order and decided the fate of nations, there were also personal gods who oversaw the lives of individual people, like the guardian angels of traditional Catholic belief. In Israel, the drive to monotheism meant that these two roles were merged: Yhwh is both the God of the whole world and the God to whom individuals can turn for protection (and, of course, whom they must fear if they transgress).

This fusion is a distinctive part of Israelite monotheism, and it was clearly already in place by the time of Amos. Religious faith today takes it for granted that God is both the ruler of the universe and the one who is concerned with each individual, and often fails to see what a remarkable combination of ideas this is. It was far from intuitively obvious to most people in the ancient world.

THEOLOGICAL ETHICS

It is not certain how far we can really talk of "theology" proper in the ancient Near East. The reflections that we encounter on the gods are seldom sufficiently developed or critical to be part of what we normally mean by the word today. Nevertheless, there were of course ideas about the divine realm, and about the gods' involvement in human affairs, outside Israel as well as within it – though Israelite thinkers went much further in analyzing the concept of the divine, and Amos, as we have seen, was among the first to do this. One thing that can be said with confidence is that theology in the world Amos inhabited was not normally closely linked with ethics, if by ethics we primarily mean the way people behave toward each other. In very general terms, the gods may have instructed kings to draw up lawcodes, as Hammurabi claims in the prologue to the great code that bears his name:

> When lofty Amun, king of the Annunaki,
> (and) Enlil, lord of heaven and earth,
> the determiner of the destinies of the land,
> determined for Marduk, the first-born of Enki,
> the Enlil functions over all mankind,
> made him great among the Igigi,
> called Babylon by its exalted name,
> made it supreme in the world,
> established for him in its midst an enduring kingship,
> whose foundations are as firm as heaven and earth –
> at that time Anum and Enlil named me
> to promote the welfare of the people,
> me, Hammurabi, the devout, god-fearing prince,
> to cause justice to prevail in the land,
> to destroy the wicked and the evil,
> that the strong might not oppress the weak…
>
> When Marduk commissioned me to guide the people aright,
> To direct the land,
> I established law and justice in the language of the land,
> Thereby promoting the welfare of the people,
> At that time I decreed:[11]
>   (*the specific laws follow*)

But there is no sense that a god concerned himself with the details of how human conduct should be regulated, still less that in

---

[11]   *ANET*, 164–165.

transgressing human ethical codes one was likely to incite the gods to anger. This was prone to happen only in the case of actions that could be defined as blasphemous or a challenge to the gods themselves. Hence, the various types of action that can be described as *hubris* – arrogating to oneself rights or privileges that properly belong to the gods alone – might cause one's downfall, as might certain "abominations" such as incest. Above all, the gods would be angered if the proper sacrifices were not offered, and this could lead the god to withdraw his or her presence from the sanctuary, which then might fall to an enemy. This is the theological background against which Amos has to be read.

We see at once that Amos – both the prophet and the book – has a different attitude from what was normal in the ancient Near East. It is assumed that Yhwh takes a close interest in human conduct: the conduct of all nations in times of war, and the behavior of individual Israelites *toward each other*. Yhwh is angered by atrocities in war, yet also by the way the rich treat the poor. His continued approval of Israel has nothing at all to do with the correct offering of sacrifices. Indeed, one of the most striking features of the book (as also of Hosea, Isaiah, and Jeremiah) is the assertion that Yhwh does not desire sacrifice at all (see Amos 3:4–5; 5:21–24; Hos 6:6; Isa 1:10–15; Jer 6:20). The principle is spelled out most famously in Micah:

> "With what shall I come before the Lord,
>   and bow myself before God on high?
> Shall I come before him with burnt-offerings,
>   with calves a year old?
> Will the Lord be pleased with thousands of rams,
>   with ten thousands of rivers of oil?
> Shall I give my firstborn for my transgression,
>   the fruit of my body for the sin of my soul?"
> He has told you, O mortal, what is good;
>   and what does the Lord require of you

> but to do justice, and to love kindness, and to walk humbly with
> your God? (Micah 6:6–8)

It would not matter how great the sacrifice was – rivers of oil or
even the sacrifice of a firstborn child – Yhwh would pay no heed.
What Yhwh is interested in is proper behavior toward other people, consisting of what we, in a shorthand phrase, normally call
"social justice." We saw in detail what this involves in Chapter 3
herein: probity in commercial and judicial practice, care for the
poor, and respect for the needs of widows, orphans, and slaves. It
is not the case that other ancient cultures did not also value these
things. But they did not link them to the gods in the way that
Amos links them to Yhwh, and they certainly did not see them as
the terms of a contract between them and the gods. Here, Amos is
strikingly original.

So, for Amos and the compilers of his book, ethics is closely connected with God. But it is not necessarily the case that God is seen
as one who *commands* certain norms. In the case of the war crimes
enumerated in chapters 1–2, for example, we seem to be dealing
with conventional, rather than divinely given, rules. Nowhere does
Amos explicitly say that God has *commanded* people to behave in
a certain way; he talks rather of "what is right" (Hebrew *nĕkōḥâ*;
Amos 3:10). But God certainly oversees the consequences of
wrong action, and avenges breaches of the moral code, much like
a human judge.

One of the most arresting points Amos makes is that God
requires (to use Hosea's words) "mercy and not sacrifice":

> I hate, I despise your festivals,
>> and I take no delight in your solemn assemblies.
> Even though you offer me your burnt-offerings
>> and grain-offerings,
> I will not accept them;

and the offerings of well-being of your fatted animals
    I will not look upon.
Take away from me the noise of your songs;
    I will not listen to the melody of your harps.
But let justice roll down like waters,
    and righteousness like an ever-flowing stream. (Amos 5:23–24)

As we have seen, this probably really does mean that God is not interested in the sacrificial cult, and prefers human justice to worship through sacrificial offerings (or even through the offering of music and song, quite an extraordinary idea). This is so remarkable that many commentators refuse to believe it, and argue that Amos really wants people to be just *as well as* to offer sacrifice, but it seems to me that the point could hardly be made more plainly that sacrifice is not desired. This is sometimes called a "Protestant" emphasis in the prophets. At times, it is asserted that such an interpretation of the prophets as against the cultus is anachronistic, a reading back by Protestants, of Protestantism, into the Old Testament. But others use the term "Protestant" to point to a perennial division within a number of religions, including Christianity, over the question of what is pleasing to God. "Protestants" in this sense classically argue that God is not concerned with outward ceremonies but with the inward dispositions of the heart, and especially with how those dispositions work themselves out in the practice of social justice. Of course, this is a major theme in modern Catholic teaching too, even as there are people who call themselves Protestants but who in practice seem all too little aware of social injustice. But the rough and ready use of the term "Protestant" for what the prophets were saying does not seem to me essentially misleading as a way of capturing the "ethics rather than ritual" aspect of the teaching of Amos. It does mark him and his prophetic successors out from the normal beliefs of ancient peoples.

How would one apply this "Protestant" emphasis today? It is important to remember that a term such as "ritual" covers a multitude of activities. The sacrifice of animals at local shrines in order to feast on them in the presence of God is not really much like the ceremonial style of worship practiced in Catholic or Orthodox traditions, neither is it like the solemn rites of modern Judaism. The thin thread connecting the two can only be found in a shared belief that God requires and desires the offering of ritual acts. But the people condemned by Amos appear to have thought that this was *all* God required of them: what a god needs is regular sacrifice, and that is the end of the story. To the contrary, there are no Jews or Christians who think that the offering of liturgy is the only thing God requires. All agree that correct personal (and indeed corporate) conduct is also needed. In that sense, the prophetic critique of Israel's ancient religious practices has hit home in all traditions in Judaism and Christianity, not only in their more "Protestant" strains. The most "ritualistic" Christian, therefore, hardly comes anywhere near the attachment of Amos's contemporaries to the sacrificial cult as (supposedly) the one and only demand made on them by God. This does not mean that there is no challenge left in the prophet's words for modern people. It is still possible to be concerned with the outside of religious things, and not to concern oneself much with justice and mercy. Where such attitudes exist, Amos provides a warning against them. St. Vincent de Paul, the founder of the Lazarists, put the point rather clearly in the seventeenth century:

> The service of the poor is to be preferred to all else, and to be performed without delay. If at a time set aside for prayer, medicine or help has to be brought to some poor person, go and do what has to be done with an easy mind, offering it up to God as a prayer. Do not be put out by uneasiness or a sense of sin because

of prayers interrupted by the service of the poor: for God is not neglected if prayers are put aside, if the work of God[12] is interrupted, in order that another such work may be completed.[13]

DIVINE ACTION

How does God act in the world? Ancient Israelites seem to have been in no doubt about this. He acts in two ways: through natural phenomena and through political and social events. In Amos, it is clear that the earthquake is the work of YHWH (Amos 9:1), as are the regular sequence of day and night and its occasional disruption by eclipse or storm. Equally clearly, the relations between nations, especially in time of war, bear witness to divine activity. YHWH uses foreign nations (the Arameans and/or Assyrians) to punish Israel, just as according to the Moabite stele Chemosh had used the house of Omri to punish the Moabites. Isaiah would continue this way of thinking about warfare with his oracle about the Assyrians (Isa 10:5–6), but it is a commonplace of ancient Near Eastern religious thought.

It is, however, very hard to accept today. Insurance policies still describe natural disasters such as earthquakes as "acts of God," but few take the term seriously: it is almost consciously archaic. Few Jews or Christians ask what the victims of natural disaster did to deserve it; most turn away in horror from such an idea.[14] And the fate of nations in war is not commonly regarded as a reflection of

---

[12] At this point, "the work of God" means the prayers of the Divine Office, the regular daily prayers of Catholic observance.

[13] From a letter of St. Vincent de Paul. See *Celebrating the Saints* (ed. R. Atwell; Norwich: Canterbury Press, 1998), 338.

[14] See further, Terence E. Fretheim, *Creation Untamed: The Bible, God, and Natural Disasters* (Grand Rapids: Baker Academic, 2010).

their merits or shortcomings. We know that victory does not always go to the deserving. If we take any recent conflict in the world, we will find it very difficult to specify where God was in defeat and where God was in victory, and we are likely to be wary of the idea that he "uses" one nation to punish another, so that nations are merely tools in his hand. There are indeed religious people who believe all these things, but they are no longer in the majority, at least not in the Western world. We still go to war for what seem to us moral reasons, but we do not suppose that God will always guarantee a just outcome, and we spend much time agonizing over all the innocent victims of even the most just war. Thus the modern world view, even among religious people, is inhospitable to the prophetic idea of how God works in the world. Amos's message describes, at best, how one might feel the world *ought* to function, but not at all how it actually does. And the editors who thought that divine action could make fine-grained distinctions between righteous and wicked when disaster befell a nation were even further from what appears to be the case than the prophet himself, who at least saw how indiscriminate disaster, natural or military, can be and so often is.

This is one issue that is not helped by a canonical perspective, since the whole Old Testament and indeed the whole Christian Bible assumes that God's purposes are worked out in the events of world history, and that the rise and fall of kingdoms reveals the favor and condemnation of God. Josephus, in the first century, put it as follows, in reference to the biblical histories:

> The main lesson to be learnt from this history [i.e., the history recounted in the historical books of the Hebrew Bible] by any who care to peruse it is that men who conform to the will of God, and do not venture to transgress laws that have been excellently laid down, prosper in all things beyond belief, and for their

reward are offered by God felicity; whereas, in proportion as they depart from the strict observance of these laws, things else practicable become impracticable, and whatever good thing they strive to do ends in irretrievable disasters.[15]

Amos would surely have agreed, and so would all those who had a hand in the book named after him. Most people before modern times saw things in the same way. We are divided from them by a huge gulf, and it is not clear how it can be bridged: the average religious person today sees matters quite differently from all the biblical writers on this point. This fact is disguised by the amount of Old Testament material that is read in the Christian churches as though everyone still agreed with it, but in fact, most people do not. One can only imagine how people would react if they were told that the Nazis had been the "rod in YHWH's hand" to punish the Jewish people, as Isaiah saw the Assyrians of his day. Such a notion would be regarded as a completely intolerable piece of theological error, so heinous indeed that even to mention it may be felt to be unacceptable. In brief, I do not see how the biblical teaching on the subject of divine action is ever to be fruitful for our theological thinking today.

Much the same applies to the biblical treatment of natural disaster as revealing the hand of God. For the Bible, it is regarded as obvious that when an event cannot be attributed to human causation, then its cause is God. We see this clearly in the story of David and the census in 2 Samuel 24. There, David is given three options in punishment for his sin in ordering the census (to which YHWH incited him anyway!): three years of famine, three months

---

[15] Josephus, *Jewish Antiquities*, 1.14; translation from Flavius Josephus, *Jewish Antiquities: Books I–III* (trans. H. St. J. Thackeray; repr. ed.; LCL; Cambridge: Harvard University Press, 1998 [orig: 1930]).

of fleeing from his foes, or three days of plague (2 Sam 24:12–13).
He rejects the second of these and leaves Yhwh to choose between
the other two, saying, "[L]et us fall into the hand of the Lord, for
his mercy is great, but let me not fall into human hands" (2 Sam
24:14) – clearly implying that famine and plague are sent directly
by God, as opposed to the human agency involved in military conflict – though in this story that is also offered by God. Similarly,
the death of David and Bathsheba's child is seen as a direct blow
by God: "the Lord struck the child that Uriah's wife bore to David,
and it became very ill" (2 Sam 12:15). Modern believers do not in
general share these beliefs, and do not see God as directly involved
in events in this way. Here, too, I do not think we can turn back
the clock.

ESCHATOLOGY

Not all agree that we should speak of "eschatology" in Amos, or
in any of the prophets, since it often seems to imply a final goal
for the world on a scale greater than they thought of – the "end of
the world." Nevertheless, the term is common in biblical studies as
referring to the sense we find in many books that Yhwh is "inau-
gurating a new action in history in relation to his people and to
the consummation of his purpose."[16] In that sense, it is reasonable
to speak of Amos's "eschatology." As we have seen, there was probably a "popular eschatology" in Amos's day according to which
Yhwh was expected to intervene decisively on behalf of Israel on
the "day of Yhwh." This was an eschatology that Amos rejected

---

[16] E. W. Heaton, *The Hebrew Kingdoms* (Oxford: Oxford University Press,
1968), 59.

and reversed, predicting instead a day of disaster. This idea of the "day" as a time of destruction for Israel continues in Isaiah and in Zephaniah and Ezekiel (Zeph 1:10–18; Ezek 7:10–12). Later additions to the book of Amos revert to the hopeful message of better times to come, so that the eschatology of the finished book is a positive one, with predictions of blessing on the nation and even on nature (Amos 9:11–15). One could compare at this point the promises in Zechariah 8:1–19 and Isaiah 65:17–25, quoted earlier in Chapter 4.

Modern believers will no doubt want to know whether God's future is to be bright or bleak, and if they turn to the prophetic books, they will thus get an ambiguous answer. The Old Testament alone certainly does not settle the matter because it contains both types of eschatology, and it is hard to choose between them – though the "final form" of the text privileges hope and blessing over destruction and despair. But Christians and Jews traditionally draw on other resources to answer questions about the future. In Christianity, the teaching of the New Testament; and in Judaism, the eschatology of the Mishnah, Talmud, and Midrashim, which, on the whole, promise blessings to Israel but envisions the possibility that individuals may be excluded from them. The New Testament perspective is not so very different. There is a larger problem, however, in appealing to Amos or any other book of the Bible for teaching about eschatology, and that is that most modern people in the West do not think in biblical terms at all about the future of the individual, the nation, the Church, the world, or the planet. Our projections of the future rest on history, sociology, economics, and science. For most Western Christians, the biblical message of coming judgment has come to be internalized as a message to the individual or to society demanding change and reform, and is no longer perceived as providing information about the future, whether short or long term.[17] This has not prevented some systematic theologians from writing about Christian hope. One thinks of Jürgen Moltmann's *Theology of Hope* or Gerhard Sauter's *What Dare We Hope?*[18] But in such works, biblical eschatologies are radically transformed into systems of thinking about God and his involvement in human affairs, not affirmed as literally true. Indeed, one might say that biblical eschatology is taken no more literally than biblical "protology" – the creation stories – in modern theology.

It remains true that many modern believers still feel the sense of challenge in Amos's eschatology – a sense that God is not indifferent to how human beings act, and will eventually direct the outcome of history in ways that take account of this. Current ecological concerns have given new life to the idea that an older liberalism thought wholly outdated, the idea that the planet might come to a devastating end one day, and that that day might not be as distant as we would hope. But bringing our current fears for universal destruction into line with biblical eschatology is difficult. For the prophets, it was not environmental issues or nuclear war that threatened the human race and its habitat, but the naked power of God, who worked with a time frame unrelated to human action in matters of ecology or technology. To argue that we now see that the biblical writers got it right after all is facile, and ignores the fact that they were thinking in categories quite different from our own.

---

[17] This is not true, of course, for the many people, particularly in North America, who espouse some form of millennialism.

[18] Jürgen Moltmann, *Theology of Hope: On the Ground and the Implications of a Christian Eschatology* (London: SCM, 1967); Gerhard Sauter, *What Dare We Hope? Reconsidering Eschatology* (Harrisburg, PA: Trinity Press International, 1999).

Further Reading

COMMENTARIES ON AMOS

Amos is well served by a host of excellent commentaries. Written from very different points of view, the following are especially recommended:

Francis I. Andersen and David N. Freedman, *Amos: A New Translation with Notes and Commentary* (AB 24A; New York: Doubleday, 1989).

Jörg Jeremias, *The Book of Amos: A Commentary* (trans. D. W. Stott; OTL; Louisville: Westminster John Knox, 1998 [German orig: 1995]).

James Luther Mays, *Amos: A Commentary* (OTL; London: SCM, 1969).

Shalom M. Paul, *Amos: A Commentary on the Book of Amos* (ed. F. M. Cross; Hermeneia; Minneapolis: Fortress, 1991).

Hans Walter Wolff, *Joel and Amos: A Commentary on the Books of the Prophets Joel and Amos* (trans. W. Janzen, S. D. McBride, Jr., and C. A. Muenchow; ed. S. D. McBride, Jr.; Hermeneia; Philadelphia: Fortress, 1977 [German orig.: 1969]).

Jeremias's work is the most up to date of these and represents the German-speaking tradition of composition criticism very well.

Wolff's work, building on previous form-critical study, has been
seminal for all study of Amos from the late 1970s onwards. Paul
stands in a very different tradition, in which it is assumed that
most of the book goes back to the prophet himself. Andersen and
Freedman is a moderate work in the Anglo-American tradition
of scholarship. For a general overview of the message of the book,
however, the older commentary of Mays can still be thoroughly
recommended.

General Studies

The best all-round book on Amos is the (untranslated) work by
Robert Martin-Achard, *Amos: l'homme, le message, l'influence*
(Geneva: Labor et Fides, 1984). As the title indicates, this includes
both a study of the prophet himself, of the book, and of its reception history – on the last point, it was very much ahead of its time.
For anyone who reads French, this is probably the best way of getting into the book of Amos. It is thoroughly informed about Amos
scholarship up to the 1980s, and engages the reader with a lively
and interesting style.

On the composition of the book, a survey of scholarly opinion
together with some original proposals can be found in Tchavdar
S. Hadjiev, *The Composition and Redaction of the Book of Amos*
(BZAW 393; Berlin: Walter de Gruyter, 2009).

On the structure of the book of Amos, see R. E. Clements,
"Patterns in the Prophetic Canon," in idem, *Old Testament Prophecy:
From Oracles to Canon* (Louisville: Westminster John Knox, 1996),
191–202; J. de Waard, "The Chiastic Structure of Amos V,1–17,"
VT 27 (1977): 170–177; Paul R. Noble, "The Literary Structure of
Amos: A Thematic Analysis," *JBL* 114 (1995): 209–226; N. J. Tromp,
"Amos V 1–17: Towards a Stylistic and Rhetorical Analysis," in
Prophets, Worship and Theodicy: Studies in Prophetism, Biblical

Theology and Structural and Rhetorical Analysis and on the Place of Music in Worship: Papers Read at the Joint British-Dutch Old Testament Conference held at Woudschoten, 1982 (OtSt 23; Leiden: Brill, 1984), 65–85; and R. Bryan Widbin, "Center Structure in the Center Oracles of Amos," in *"Go to the Land I Will Show You": Studies in Honor of Dwight W. Young* (eds. J. E. Coleson and V. H. Matthews; Winona Lake: Eisenbrauns, 1996), 177–192.

On the theology of Amos, useful works include John Barton, "The Theology of Amos," in *Prophecy and the Prophets in Ancient Israel: Proceedings of the Oxford Old Testament Seminar* (ed. John Day; LHBOTS 531; London: T & T Clark, 2010), 188–201; idem, *Amos's Oracles against the Nations* (SOTSMS 6; Cambridge: Cambridge University Press, 1980), reprinted in idem, *Understanding Old Testament Ethics* (Louisville: Westminster John Knox, 2003); Hans M. Barstad, *The Religious Polemics of Amos: Studies in the Preaching of Am. 2,7B-8; 4,1–13; 5,1–27; 6,4–7; 8,14* (VTSup 34; Leiden: Brill 1984); Brevard S. Childs, *Introduction to the Old Testament as Scripture* (Philadelphia: Fortress, 1979), 395–410; Léon Epsztein, *Social Justice in the Ancient Near East and the People of the Bible* (trans. J. Bowden; London: SCM, 1986 [French orig: 1983]); Karl Möller, *A Prophet in Debate: The Rhetoric of Persuasion in the Book of Amos* (JSOTSup 372; Sheffield: Sheffield Academic Press, 2003); and A. Vanlier Hunter, *Seek the Lord! A Study of the Meaning and Purpose of the Exhortations in Amos, Hosea, Isaiah, Micah, and Zephaniah* (Baltimore: St Mary's Seminary & University, 1982).

On the place of Amos in the prophetic corpus see Paul R. House, *The Unity of the Twelve* (JSOTSup 97; Sheffield: Sheffield Academic Press, 1990); James Nogalski, *Literary Precursors to the Book of the Twelve* (BZAW 217; Berlin: Walter de Gruyter, 1993); and (for a contrary view) Ehud Ben Zvi, "Twelve Prophetic Books or 'The

Twelve'? A Few Preliminary Considerations," in *Forming Prophetic Literature: Essays on Isaiah and the Twelve in Honor of John D. W. Watts* (eds. J. W. Watts and P. R. House; JSOTSup 235; Sheffield: Sheffield Academic Press, 1996), 125–156.

For a survey of writing on Amos down to 1998, see Roy F. Melugin, "Amos in Recent Research," *CurBS* 6 (1998): 65–101.

Author Index

Scripture and Apocrypha Index